FIND Y
LIFE
PURPOSE

**THE SECRET FOR A
SUCCESSFUL AND HAPPY LIFE**

o o o

MERVYN SMALLWOOD

PURPOSEFUL BOOKS

First published in 2012 by Purposeful Books, Cornwall, UK.
http://www.PurposefulBooks.com

Copyright © 2012 Mervyn Smallwood
http://www.MervynSmallwood.com

All rights reserved. No part of this publication may be reproduced, stored or transmitted in any form without prior permission from the copyright owner.

ISBN 978-0-9574713-0-6

The personal stories included in this book are true to life and have either been written with the person's permission or are composites of real situations where details have been changed sufficiently to protect the identity of the individuals concerned. Any resemblance to people either living or dead is coincidental.

Cover design, layout and typesetting by
Alison Rayner, London, UK.

o o o

CONTENTS

∘ ∘ ∘

PREFACE: Why This Book?.. 1

INTRODUCTION: Why Finding Your Life Purpose Will Make You Happy and Successful.. 7

STEP 1: See Life Afresh 31

STEP 2: Do Something Worthwhile 59

STEP 3: Tune Into Your Soul 81

STEP 4: Wake Up To Your Dreams 103

STEP 5: Play To Your Strengths 125

STEP 6: Plan Your Way Forward....................................149

STEP 7: Prepare For Success 179

AFTERWORD: Living Every Day in Pursuit of Your Purpose 205

ADDITIONAL RESOURCES 208

ABOUT THE AUTHOR 209

ACKNOWLEDGEMENTS 210

BIBLIOGRAPHY 211

∘ ∘ ∘

PREFACE
Why This Book?

○ ○ ○

AS YOU'VE PICKED UP THIS BOOK I believe it's more than mere coincidence. There's a reason why you're reading this. Whether you've already been searching for a while, or are just mildly curious, or it seems you've stumbled across this almost by accident, what you've got here is the answer to the question, "What is the secret for a successful and happy life?" I believe it's found in discovering and living out your unique purpose in life.

My own search for purpose began in my early twenties. Having achieved two major goals in life much sooner than expected, life turned hollow. Achieving goals didn't give me the satisfaction I sought. I then took up martial arts and became interested in the philosophy and spirituality behind them, spending hours in meditation and study. My journey led me through Buddhism, Taoism, Shintoism, Confucianism, Hinduism, Christianity, New-Age thinking and more. For thirty years I've read countless books, attended seminars, sought out gurus to learn from, experimented, and spent much time in personal reflection. It's been my life quest. Along the way I've tried to help others, becoming a qualified life coach and also an ordained church minister. Please hear me out. I'm not going to tell you, "You've gotta get religion." I've seen how religion has caused problems for some and got God a bad name. Finally, I reached a place of peace and understanding – something I'm sure you can do too.

So why this book? I know you've heard it before, but this book is different. I've read many of the books out there that talk about life, meaning and purpose. While all helped a bit, for me they still missed something; they couldn't seem to scratch where I itched. Some books encouraged me to just choose a dream and go for it; others told me God had a set plan and I had to follow it. As I grappled with issues such as

PREFACE

having a preset destiny, a calling or a choice in life; focusing inwardly on myself or outwardly on serving others; I gradually pieced together principles that helped me find my life purpose – and can help you too.

I've put this book together in a certain way. I think you'll find it easier if you start at the beginning and work through it step by step. First, the introduction explains how you can benefit from finding and living your life's purpose. Next, step one lays a foundation as you look at life from a different perspective. Then step two helps you discover what's meaningful to you. Step three puts you back in touch with your inner guidance system. Four explores your hopes and dreams. Five helps you decide what to do with your strengths, skills and abilities. Six helps you craft a plan for the future. Seven prepares you for the challenges you may face as you seek to live out your newly clarified purpose. Finally there's a few thoughts on living every day in pursuit of your purpose plus some information on additional resources should you wish to learn more.

Finding your purpose is a process that will take a bit of time and effort. Following the steps outlined above will guide you on your journey. Sometimes what you read will trigger new thoughts and open up possibilities. At other times you will find yourself tightening up on your focus. This book will equip you with what you need to find your own purpose in life. One of the main ways it helps you do this is by leading you through a series of exercises.

ooooooooooooooooooooooooooooooooooooooooo

EXERCISES

Each chapter has a number of simple yet powerful exercises. They'll all be highlighted separately like this. These help you apply what you're learning about to your own life. Some are very quick; others need a bit of thinking about. They are designed to help you gain deeper insight and also to prompt you to take action. It's through doing something different you will make progress on your journey.

ooooooooooooooooooooooooooooooooooooooooo

FIND YOUR LIFE PURPOSE

I'd encourage you to get a special notebook or file where you can capture what comes to mind as you work through the exercises. If you can, find something that fits in your pocket so you can carry it with you. This way you can take it out and reflect on what you've written from time to time. Also, you can use it to jot down any other thoughts you might have as you go along.

I won't promise to completely transform your life in just seven days – though if you read this book in a week and apply what you learn you could do exactly that. Instead, what I'm offering is a practical guide to help you discover and live out your unique purpose in life. It's this that will provide you with real happiness, lasting fulfilment and true success. If a journey of a thousand miles begins with a single step, the next step forward in the discovery of your life purpose can be found simply by turning the page...

○ ○ ○

INTRODUCTION

WHY FINDING YOUR LIFE PURPOSE WILL MAKE YOU HAPPY AND SUCCESSFUL

○ ○ ○

INTRODUCTION
Why Finding Your Life Purpose Will Make You Happy and Successful

○ ○ ○

"I can't get no satisfaction!"
(Mick Jagger – Rolling Stones)

○ ○ ○

Searching for satisfaction

MICK JAGGER WAS ONTO SOMETHING. He'd already achieved fame and fortune but he knew something was missing from his life. What was it that eluded him? He wanted what we all want – to be truly happy. He was searching for that something that would give him lasting satisfaction. The trouble was, he couldn't find it.

How about you? Are you *truly* happy? Do you have *lasting* satisfaction? If not, just like Mick Jagger, you must be missing something too. Without finding that something you will always have that strange feeling inside. Some call it an inner frustration, others say it's like part of them is searching for an answer – though they can't always explain what the question is.

What had Mick and his friends experimented with in their search for satisfaction? Being wealthy they'd already enjoyed many of the things money could buy. They could afford nice houses, nice cars and nice clothes. Quickly becoming one of the world's most popular bands, they won the attention of others and achieved a level of fame the rest of us could only dream about. And there's probably more they could have enjoyed from their privileged position. Yet this still didn't bring the longed-for satisfaction.

INTRODUCTION

I believe these guys were serious in their pursuit of happiness. It seems they'd put a lot of effort into their search. You pick up a clue from the song as it goes on to say, "Cause I try and I try and I try and I try." They had riches, recognition and relationships. But even after all that effort Mick concludes the song saying in the end these things alone give "no satisfaction, no satisfaction, no satisfaction".

○○○

EXERCISE: Searching for satisfaction
Look back over your life. Where have you been searching for satisfaction? What was it that you believed would make you happy? To what extent did these things live up to your expectations? Make a note of your thoughts in your notebook or file.

○○○

Why pursuing pleasure won't make you happy

Many people believe that lasting satisfaction comes from experiencing pleasure on an ongoing basis. For some this sense of pleasure comes from acquiring possessions, for others they seek it out in relationships. Food and drink can be the focus of attention for many while achieving a position of power satisfies others. However, it's not the object itself that is pleasurable, it's the feelings you get from pursuing and obtaining it that provides the pleasure. Getting what you want and achieving your goals can give you an adrenaline rush that feels good at the time. The danger is you can fall into a trap of always wanting more. In between the highs of having your desires satisfied, you can experience lows and a sense of dissatisfaction. You can become addicted to these highs and the result is you can be caught up in a continual chase for more.

Modern marketing is often built on the idea that it's completely normal for you to be pursuing pleasure. Messages such as, "This can be yours... you owe it to yourself" and "Enjoy the pleasure of..." bombard us every day. It's as if there's an underlying message that life should be an unbroken experience of unceasing and increasing happiness. However, this promise of living a life filled with permanent pleasure can be deceiving. When life fails to live up to our expectations we become disillusioned. As one public speaker I've previously heard put it, "We become disillusioned because we have believed an illusion in the first place." Have you ever wondered where the suggestion came from that we should be continually happy?

Hedonism comes from the Greek word "hedone", meaning pleasure. A hedonistic lifestyle simply means to pursue pleasure. Popular in early Greek and Roman cultures, sensual indulgence was valued more than anything else. Pain was to be avoided; pleasure was to be pursued. Life was very much focused on enjoying the here and now. For many, consequences and the afterlife were given scant attention. The ancient saying of "eat, drink and be merry for tomorrow we die" focused on living for today while conveniently overlooking tomorrow. A hedonistic viewpoint encourages people to be self-centred and live by the motto, "If it feels good, do it!" I sometimes wonder if society has changed much in the past 2,000 years.

Though it seems hedonism has remained popular throughout history, this self-serving mindset has been challenged from time to time. During the period in which hedonism was on the rise Epicurus, the Greek philosopher, suggested that instead of pursuing physical pleasures people should seek inner tranquillity and freedom from fear. Closer to our time, John Stuart Mill, the British politician and philosopher, published a book in 1863 entitled *Utilitarianism*. Mill ranked pleasures in a hierarchical order with physical pleasure sitting well below intellectual, cultural and spiritual pleasures. This led him to conclude that the most valuable pursuits were those that brought the greatest level of happiness to the largest number of people in society. Starting out as a self-centred hedonist, over time Mill ended up becoming more of a kind-hearted altruist. As he served others for their benefit and well-being, he found

INTRODUCTION

that this made him happier than living first and foremost for himself. Within *Utilitarianism* Mill wrote, "According to the Greatest Happiness Principle... the ultimate end is an existence as far as possible from pain, and as rich as possible in enjoyments, both in point of quantity and quality." However, he concluded this was best demonstrated when enjoyments were "to the greatest extent possible, secured to all mankind; and not to them only, but, as far as the nature of things admits, to the whole sentient creation".

There's nothing immoral with acquiring wealth and experiencing pleasure. In fact, most of us would probably think there's something wrong if we came across someone who said, "My aim is to become poor and unhappy." In our efforts to become wealthy and happy what we need to look at is our motives and expectations. If we think these things will continue to provide us with the happiness we're after then it's likely that at some point we'll become disillusioned. Wealth and pleasure alone cannot provide us with the lasting satisfaction we so desperately seek.

In her recent book on *The Selfish Society*, British psychotherapist Sue Gerhardt concludes, "In the West, we have acquired so much stuff, but it has failed to make people feel good inside. On the contrary, it has made us increasingly depressed." Dissatisfaction levels in modern society appear to be higher than we would have expected a generation ago. Further research carried out by the University of Warwick has shown a noticeable decline in human happiness within developed countries during the very period they have enjoyed increased financial wealth. Andrew Oswald, a professor within the team, asked himself, "What is it that goes wrong in a country as it gets richer?" After all his research he confessed, "We do not yet know." One main recommendation they came out with from the study was that, "We should now be measuring a nation's emotional prosperity more than its economic prosperity (ie we ought to focus on the level of mental well-being, not on the number of pounds in people's bank accounts)."

Whereas pursuing and experiencing pleasure might make you feel happy, there's no guarantee it will last. Happiness can be elusive; it's there one minute and gone the next. You need more than this. You need to find the source of lasting satisfaction. You won't find it in things that money can buy. If you want to satisfy your hunger for happiness at the deepest level you need to be looking elsewhere.

Striving for success

Having read many books and listened to a number of speakers on the subject of success, I've noticed they often refer back to a handful of influential thinkers. These include people like Napoleon Hill who wrote *Think and Grow Rich*; Norman Vincent Peale who challenged us with *The Power of Positive Thinking*; and W Clement Stone who promised us *Success through a Positive Mental Attitude*. Interestingly, when you look at their backgrounds you find they developed their thinking during a period of history when people were working hard to rebuild their lives and countries following severe trials. Such ordeals included The Great Depression in America and the wider-reaching Second World War. With this in mind, it's easy to see why they would strive with almost superhuman effort to achieve what many would consider almost impossible. It doesn't seem logical to tell people they can become rich when the whole country is experiencing a recession or depression. Yet that's what Napoleon Hill did and many attest to achieving success through following the principles he laid out in his book.

If you want to achieve your goals and increase your wealth then these classics still provide you with some practical guiding principles. Over the years, many have applied the lessons learned from these books and built great empires. Their businesses have provided products, services and employment for others. We should be thankful for all their hard work. Sadly though, some of these empires have also collapsed and their owners died broke and disheartened people. If success is measured in terms of building businesses and personal wealth then it can be both gained and also lost.

INTRODUCTION

Many years ago there lived a man who had everything a man could want for. He was the richest man on earth with a wealth that exceeded that of John D Rockefeller, Andrew Carnegie and Bill Gates combined. Many people would call him lucky because he was born into wealth; he never had to work a day of his life if he didn't want to. His father had done the hard work and he was now profiting from it. He wasn't daft either and quickly built a worldwide reputation for being the wisest person alive. A prolific author, he wrote many books, some of which still sit alongside today's best-sellers. In his time and culture, success could also be measured by the number of wives a man had. This man beat all previous known records by building up a harem of 300 wives plus 700 concubines. Can you imagine that? In case you are wondering, this man was Solomon, king of Israel, who reigned from 971-931BC.

Here was a man who amassed so much gold that silver lost its value and became a commonplace decorative building material. The respect he commanded from others resulted in foreign kings and queens travelling hundreds of miles overland just to hear him speak –before the days of paved roads. And to top it all he could sleep with a different woman every night of the week if he wanted to. No man on earth ever had as much as Solomon and I doubt if any other man ever will. Yet if you read what he wrote you discover something shocking; this still didn't provide Solomon with the lasting satisfaction he sought. The man who had everything we associate with worldly success revealed that he still felt a sense of lack. "Meaningless, meaningless, utterly meaningless" is how he described life even with all his wealth, wisdom and women. He discovered that being rich and famous, having all the possessions you could want and holding a position of great power, you can still feel like you are missing something in your search for inner satisfaction.

Measuring success

People often equate success with acquiring wealth, enjoying the popularity of others or some great achievement. To become successful in this way can sometimes take a lot of effort. Athletes push themselves through gruelling training routines day in and day out, year after year, just so they can beat others by the narrowest of margins. Through doing so they win the accolades and adoration of fans. However, when someone else comes along who is only a tenth of a second faster, their previous success is often overshadowed and can even become forgotten. Only those who were the first to do something others thought was impossible are remembered for longer. Sir Roger Bannister is known for breaking the four-minute mile barrier in 1954. But have you heard of John Landy who also ran the mile in less than four minutes only two months later? Or how about Hicham El Guerrouj who in 1999 set the current record for running a mile in just three minutes and 43.13 seconds? Many went on to beat Sir Roger's time yet few are remembered for long.

When it comes to money, people without it worry about how to get it; people with it worry about how to keep it. Financial wealth can take years to build up but sometimes only moments to lose. I've known several business owners who have been forced into bankruptcy through no fault of their own. And even if you can hang on to your wealth until the end, you can't take it with you. When you pass from this life on earth, what use is a tombstone engraved with the words, "I made a fortune on earth, but I've not got a penny of it now." Is that success?

Today's materialistic society seems to stimulate a continual lust for more. New and improved products are being announced all the time. They promise greater pleasure and happiness. The danger is we then become dissatisfied with what we already have. Have you ever taken a test drive in a new car? What do you say to yourself once you get back to your old one? "Hmmm. This old car's looking a bit tired by comparison. It's scratched, more noisy, less comfortable and doesn't smell as new as what I've just driven." You've become dissatisfied. And just supposing you managed to buy that new Mercedes. When you next visit the golf club and your golfing partner pulls up in a new Ferrari do you still feel as successful?

INTRODUCTION

If you measure success in terms of the wealth you amass or the possessions you acquire, I'm sorry but I think you're fooling yourself. You're measuring the wrong things. You're saying your life can be summed up by a row of numbers on a bank statement. I don't think that's the best way to put a value on your life.

Some who have achieved fame, fortune and personal goals have stopped to question whether this is the best way to measure success. They found that the level of happiness doesn't always increase in direct proportion to the amount of prosperity or popularity they acquire. Psychiatrist and author Willard Gaylin observed, "When men achieve the fruits of their material success, they often become aware of an emptiness – an incompleteness – in their lives." I experienced this to some extent in my early twenties and this is what triggered my search for greater meaning and purpose in life.

The younger generation have been watching us who are older and can see we've been chasing after fool's gold. Too many of us have become cash-rich but time-poor. We've deceived ourselves by believing the lie that what we're doing is for the betterment of our families. The trouble is we've been so busy working that time has raced by, our children have grown up, flown the family nest – and we never really got to know them. These young people have questioned whether this is the best pattern of life to follow, come to their own conclusions, and are starting a counter-revolution. Having become disenchanted with the magic spell that we fell under, they've realized there's more to life than money, possessions and an ego-boosting job title. The emerging generation are now looking for something different. What they want isn't more materialism but meaning; they want to do something with their lives that focuses less on generating wealth and more on doing something worthwhile. According to research carried out by Common Purpose UK, 87 per cent of the young adults they surveyed want to find a career that would add purpose to their lives. In their report *Searching for Something* one of their key findings suggests, "A quarter-life crisis is a reality for young people today, and it is a time when they evaluate what they're doing and what they want from life."

Looking for happiness and success but in the right places

If you want to be happy and successful you've got to be looking in the right places. If the younger generation are looking for more meaning and purpose then they're onto something. They're starting to look in the right direction. They know that this is more important than just landing a well-paid job.

When it comes to deciding if you're successful or not you have two choices: either you can let others tell you when they think you've achieved it, or you can decide for yourself. Which one do you have control over? Other people's opinions can be encouraging in confirming what you already believe to be true. However, you should not rely upon them to set the bar against which you judge yourself. A big danger of relying on the opinions of others is that they can change over time. It also depends on who you ask. You could find yourself in a state of uncertainty, continually trying to find out if you've reached their standard or not. So my advice is to ignore others when it comes to judging whether you're successful or not. Set yourself free from any self-imposed burden you've been struggling under. You can choose your own criteria for deciding whether you are successful or not. Don't let yourself be shackled again by the opinion of others.

If you measured success in terms of achievement then it seems logical to set yourself goals and work towards them. If you believed that becoming a millionaire would prove you are a success, and you made it, you could call that a success. However, someone else could interpret success as having earned enough to pay the bills every month. So different people can have different standards for measuring success. But these attempts to measure success in an objective way still seem to be missing something.

INTRODUCTION

Another way of looking at success is more subjective. Who would you judge to be more successful: a millionaire business-woman who is overly stressed with work and doesn't see her kids as much as she'd like, or a manual worker who just makes a living, enjoys his work and sleeps well every night? I'd suggest peace of mind and inner contentment are more valuable than money. I'm not saying they're mutually exclusive because they aren't, you can have both. However, if you had to choose between a fat bank balance accompanied by a life full of stress, or doing something you enjoy while making just enough to live on, which would you honestly choose?

Another word has entered the dictionary within our generation: downshifting. Polly Ghazi and Judy Jones wrote a book about it. In *Getting a Life: The Downshifter's Guide to Happier Simpler Living* they pick up on this trend and tell how an increasing number of people are turning away from a lifestyle of materialism and seeking new ways to live a more meaningful and fulfilling life:

> *We aren't so sure now whether the twin gods of capitalism and rampant consumerism have landed us quite where we want to be. Perhaps more than ever before, we are wondering what life is all about, what it's for. We are searching for meaning and balance. Many are turning to alternative ways of living, and downshifting is one of them. Indeed, in western societies downshifting is one of the fastest-developing social trends of the late 1990s, as more of us yearn for simpler, more fulfilling lives and the time to enjoy the good things in life.*

Downshifting doesn't mean giving up on everything; it's about getting a better balance in life. It's about choosing to go after more quality of life rather than quantity in life. Sure, there are some who would take it to the extreme and seek to be self-sufficient and live off the land in a tepee. For many though it's about getting out of the rat race, focusing more on those things which matter most and living life more purposefully. A common theme from the stories in Polly and Judy's book is that downshifters take responsibility for their lives and define what success means for them. Following their decision to live more purposeful lives, they consistently report an increase in their levels of happiness. I'm not saying you have to become a downshifter. What I am saying is you can learn a lesson from them in terms of making a conscious decision to focus on what's most important in life and to define success in your own terms. This is essential if you want to discover true and lasting happiness.

EXERCISE: Measuring success
When have you felt most successful in life? How did you define success at that time? Has your understanding of what it means to be successful changed over time? In light of what we've just looked at, how successful would you say your life is right now? What would you like to change about your life to give you a greater sense of success as you now see it?

How to find real happiness

So where should you look to discover real happiness? What is it that can give you a sense of true success? How can you find a feeling of fulfilment that will last you for the rest of your life? If fame, fortune and fun fails to deliver on its promises, there's got to be something else, something that can satisfy your hunger for happiness. Otherwise, why are there so many people still searching for it?

Mick Jagger and his friends were looking for it but John Stuart Mill had already found a key to it a hundred years earlier. Having studied comparatively wealthy, successful and yet still unhappy people, Sue Gerhardt, Andrew Oswald and Willard Gaylin have also tried steering us away from mere achievement and materialism and towards a more emotionally healthier lifestyle. Having suggested you're unlikely to find it through acquiring wealth, possessions or by hopping from one

INTRODUCTION

pleasurable experience to another for the rest of your life, I'll tell you what I believe. Real happiness, lasting satisfaction and a feeling of living a successful life has to engage you at the deepest level. What I and many others have found is this:

"A truly happy and successful life comes from finding and living out your unique purpose in life."

It makes sense when you think about it. Temporary pleasures bring temporary happiness. If you're looking for something that will last your lifetime it needs to be more permanent. Whenever you try to satisfy your hunger for happiness with possessions or pleasures there's a risk. When you can't get what you want, or if you get side-tracked by the lure of bigger, better or more elsewhere, you become dissatisfied with what you have. Then your happiness level plummets. By contrast, when you become absorbed in doing something you believe is worthwhile and are passionate about, any sense of inner emptiness and frustration you may have just disappears. The trick is to work out what it is you feel is really worth giving your life for. It's doing this that will give you the sense of satisfaction you're after. Once you've found it I'd say you've found your life purpose. The way I'd define your life purpose is like this:

"Your life purpose is your unique reason for being, expressed through who you are and what you do."

That's what the rest of this book is about. It explains how you can find and live out your life purpose through using a step-by-step approach. You'll learn more about who you are and explore what you might want to do with the rest of your life. As well as recognizing what you're already good at, you'll be encouraged to think about other things you'd like to become good at. You'll also give time to working out what's really worthwhile in your own life.

Now you may have heard the saying, "You are a human being, not a human doing." It seems to have become more popular in recent years, especially in the sphere of self-development. I'd agree there's definitely some truth hidden in the heart of this statement. In this output-driven society there's been so much emphasis on what people do that sometimes who they are as individuals can be overlooked. Because of this imbalance many life coaches spend time working with their clients to help them rediscover who they really are.

While I'd agree that you should see yourself as a human being first and then as a human doing second, I'd also say you can't separate the two; you need both. Who you are is important and so is what you do. What you do should be an expression of who you are. It seems sensible to me to say you are both a human being, and a human doing. Jack Canfield also recognizes this link in relation to being, doing and purpose. He says:

> *I believe each of us is born with a life purpose. Identifying, acknowledging, and honouring this purpose is perhaps the most important action successful people take. They take the time to understand what they're here to do – and then they pursue that with passion and enthusiasm.*

Most people I've met on this journey seem to discover who they are first, then they work out what they want to do with their lives. Sometimes though you come across those who are so engrossed in what they do that's it's only when they take time out to reflect on it they discern afresh who they really are. Either way around, this book will help you get to know yourself better and guide you to find what it is that's worth your while doing in life.

○○○○○○○○○○○○○○○○○○○○○○○○○○○○○○○○○○○○○○○

EXERCISE: Human being or human doing?
Which sums up your life to date: living as a human doing or a human being? Have you found the right balance for you? Is your doing an expression of your being? If not, what do you want to do about it?

○○○○○○○○○○○○○○○○○○○○○○○○○○○○○○○○○○○○○○○

INTRODUCTION

Some benefits you'll get from finding and living out your life purpose

I've already said that by living your life aligned with your purpose you will be happier. But how? Well, here are a few thoughts...

By finding your life purpose you will put an end to the inner striving and questioning you feel about what you should be doing with your life. Instead, you will regain a sense of peace and certainty. You will experience an inner assurance, knowing you're doing the right thing. This will be especially useful when you come across others who don't understand you or what you're trying to achieve. You'll also attract others to you who share a similar passion for the things that you're focused on. And if the path you're walking seems lonely at times, you'll feel reassured that you really are heading in the right direction. You'll know that what you've given up your life for is worthwhile. Your time won't be wasted in the pursuit of things which can't give you lasting satisfaction. You'll be ready to leap out of bed in the mornings with a child-like excitement, even when you're in your sixties or seventies. You'll experience a feel good factor, knowing you've made the world a better place though your special contribution. You'll be able to look back on your life and know you've done what you were here to do. You'll know your life will not have been wasted, but invested.

If that's the kind of life you're looking for then I'd encourage you to press on and find your life purpose. You too can experience these benefits. But before I explain how you can do this I feel I need to address something. If you're like me, you may have noticed there are many who don't seem to be living a purposeful, fulfilling and happy life. Why is this?

Why so few find their purpose

First of all, I think there are many who don't make the effort to seek out their life's purpose in the first place. This could be because they've never really thought about it. Life may be so full of other things they don't seem to have the time to think. They could be caught up in things like working to make ends meet, caring for the family or following a sport or interest. None of these are bad, it's just that sometimes they take so much of our time and attention that they blind us to seeing there is more to life than daily, weekly and monthly routines.

Then there are others who may have thought about it but are not sure where to start. If we want to go somewhere different in life, we usually find it easier if we have a guide in some shape or form. If I'm travelling to a new place I get the roadmap out and study it. I'm usually starting from a place of familiarity, like home, and moving to a place of unfamiliarity, as in my chosen destination. A roadmap shows me the terrain and I plan my route accordingly. If you use a satellite navigation system (sat-nav) you've probably got more faith than me. You just dial in the destination postcode and trust that it'll tell you where to go step by step. Perhaps I'm old-school on this one, but I like to consider my journey and see where I'm going before I set off. Sometimes I pick the quickest road, other times I look for the scenic route, and there may be times when I choose a bit of both. Either way, road map or sat-nav, someone's already been there and can point you in the right direction. If you're not sure which way to go, finding a guide (like this book) can help you.

In the past I've run some Business Mastermind Groups. Within these, I've noticed how those with less experience in the business world look up to those who have more. It's natural to seek out people who've got to where we want to be so we can learn from them. Travelling from one end of my country to the other, or across the continent of Europe, is something I'd feel confident about. Give me a map and I'll be off. However, if I was thinking of trekking the Himalayas I'd seriously consider hiring a guide. I'd feel more confident that way. I've read of and met many successful people who attribute a great deal of their success to finding a coach or mentor who can help them get to where they want to be. But a good coach or mentor isn't just someone who is qualified by having got there; they've also learned how to support others on their own journey.

INTRODUCTION

Many people fail to make progress because they aren't taking advantage of the help they could get from people who've already got there.

I like to read. I was once challenged by a saying, "In ten years time you'll be the same person you are today apart from the books you read and the people you spend time with." There is a wealth of knowledge contained within books. You can gain a university-level education through regular visits to your local library. When it comes to finding and living out your life purpose you can also learn by reading the stories of others. (I'll be including insights from some of these in the following chapters.) There are times though when I've wanted to progress more quickly and I've sought out others to learn from. I've hired coaches to help me with my own development in the past. I've not seen this as a cost but as an investment. They've helped me get to where I wanted to be quicker, with less effort, and also helped me avoid some obstacles along the way. If you want to progress more quickly or can see the benefit of walking with someone who's a bit more experienced then I'd encourage you to seek out a coach who can help you.

Occasionally I meet people in life who don't venture far on their journey of discovery because of fear. They are afraid that once they set foot on this path it will lead them to a place they might not want to go. They fear they may be challenged to give up their current way of life, or that their searching will affect their closest relationships, or even that it could totally change them as a person. While this may be true for some, generally, the fear is far worse than the reality. When I've met and worked with people who have tackled this issue, I've found that they emerged the other side far more self-confident and at peace within themselves and with the world around them. I'll be looking at the issue of fear and how to overcome it in a later chapter. But before I leave this subject, if this is something affecting you I'd like to ask you a question. What's worse, living an unfulfilled life bound by fear, or facing your fears, pushing through them, and discovering the joy of living a purpose-filled and rewarding life?

There's something else I've found when talking about subjects like purpose and meaning. When some start thinking about these huge issues in life they become confused and feel overwhelmed. There is a temptation to think that you've got to be able to figure out everything before any of it can make sense. From my experience I'd say that's not necessarily the case. You can get clarity regarding your life purpose even if you are unclear about the meaning of life itself.

At this stage it may help to clarify something: the meaning of life is different to your life's purpose. The meaning of life answers the question, "Why do we (humanity) exist?" Your life's purpose answers the question, "Why do I (as an individual) exist?" Your view on the meaning of life helps you make more sense of the world around you. Recognizing your purpose helps you plan and steer a course through life, even if the world around you doesn't always make sense.

Many people look to philosophy, spirituality and religion to find an answer to the meaning of life. (We'll take a brief look at this in the next chapter.) I've met people who are clear in their mind about what they believe the meaning of life is and yet still feel unclear as to their individual purpose. I've also come across others who struggle to explain their view on the meaning of life but are very clear about describing their individual purpose. Because this is such a big issue for some, I'm also writing an accompanying book which can help you answer the question, "What is the meaning of life?"

Whether you have settled the issue of meaning or not, reading through the steps and doing the exercises provided in this book will still help you find your purpose.

How you can find your life's purpose

Some people discover their purpose by accident, others through focused effort. It may take years for some to reach a conclusion while a sudden flash of inspiration enables others to see it in an instant. Agnes found

INTRODUCTION

her purpose as a child in her parents' home as they gave hospitality to those less fortunate than themselves. She pursued this as her life's work and purpose and became a household name. Jane lived nearly fifty years before things slotted into place for her. You'll read more about Agnes and Jane in the next chapter when we talk about getting a clearer perspective in life. From reflecting on these two examples I've realized you're never too old or too young to discover your purpose in life. And even if it comes to you as a progressive revelation, you won't find it without making the initial effort.

Personally, it took me years to assemble the pieces of the jigsaw puzzle together until things made sense. It was as if someone had hidden the lid of the puzzle box that displayed the full picture. Since then I've invested many more years into study, reflection and working with others before I was able to develop the seven-step process as set out in the rest of this book.

You could follow my original path, which meandered through a range of philosophies, religions, self-development theories and practices before I found what I'd been looking for. If you've got thirty years to spare I'm happy to point you in a similar direction. Or you could create your own route and series of experiments until you (hopefully) come up with a conclusion. Alternatively, you could take the short-cut and benefit from both my experience and that of others by reading and applying what you can learn from this book. This way you're likely to find your life purpose more quickly, more easily and with less expense than I did.

The intensity of your search could vary with time. It may be the demands of everyday life, work, friends and family leave you little time to give to thinking about life and your purpose within it. If that's the case then make the most of the brief windows of opportunity you have. If you can, find a regular time you can set aside just for yourself. Some people find that first thing in the morning works best for them. Others leave it until last thing at night once the children are in bed and there's nothing else that needs doing. Maybe you have the opportunity to invest a bit more time. If you're single, or the kids have grown up and left home, you may be able to focus your attention without the risk of so many distractions. One thing I've found in life is that generally, the more effort you put into something the more you progress with it. Seeking to understand and live out your life purpose is no exception.

Herminia Ibarra wrote an interesting article for the Harvard Business Review talking about *How to Stay Stuck in the Wrong Career*. In it she said:

> *Finding one's mission in life cannot be accomplished overnight. It takes time, perseverance and hard work. But effort isn't enough; a sound method and the skill to put it into practice are also required.*

To some extent I'd agree. It took a lot of effort before I managed to reach a conclusion. One of the main reasons was that I didn't have a method to follow nor the skills required to work through the issues. Years later, I've distilled my research into a method that I believe will help you and have sought to refine the skills needed to support others. Don't panic if along the way you experience feelings of confusion, frustration or despair. These are quite normal for some as they work through issues before they get to see the way forward more clearly. What you are working on here is so significant I'd be surprised if you didn't find it challenging at times. But the results will be more than worth it.

How this book will help you find your life purpose

A book of this size would probably take an average person about six hours to read. If you do the exercises (which I'd strongly encourage you to do) then you could easily double this. If you set aside just twenty minutes every day you'd probably get through it all in about six weeks. There are quite a few self-development specialists who say it takes about

INTRODUCTION

six weeks to achieve a major change and form new, lasting habits in life. Therefore, this could be one way to approach it. Alternatively, you could step up the pace and get through it a lot quicker. If you didn't have anything else that demanded your attention you could probably read the book and complete the exercises in a weekend. This is the high-impact approach but it's not for the faint-hearted. If you try this, be aware you may hit on an issue that stops you in your tracks and requires you to give it some time to work through before you can come out the other side.

Like I said before, the more time and effort you invest in this the more you'll get out of it. Most of the exercises are based on self-reflection, I'm going to ask you to think about things and again I'd suggest you jot down your answers in a notebook. Being able to go back over your thoughts at a later time can be really helpful. There will be a few exercises where I'm going to encourage you to get feedback from others. You could tell them you're reading a book about finding purpose in life and it's made you stop and think and as a valued friend you'd really welcome their opinion. There may be a few times you'd like to go off and do some further research of your own. Check out the bibliography at the end or go to the website www.FindYourLifePurpose.com where you'll find some more information.

Please be reassured, you don't have to do any complicated maths. The exercises are also straightforward, even though they make you think. You can't fail at this either. There isn't an exam at the end and just because someone else works through the exercises and comes out with a different answer doesn't mean they're right and you're wrong. We are all individuals and we each have our own pathway to follow in discovering our unique purpose. You've already taken your first step by reading this chapter. I'd guess you've been challenged to think about a few things and gained some new insights too. It doesn't stop here though, there's so much more to learn. You'll continue your journey in the next chapter as you learn to see life from a clearer perspective. Before you move on though, I'd like to quickly summarize some key thoughts from what you've just read.

> ## Key thoughts to take away:
>
> Key thoughts to take away from this chapter include:
>
> - Temporary pleasures can't provide lasting satisfaction
>
> - Wealth, popularity and achievements aren't the best measure of success
>
> - Younger people are experiencing a quarter-life crisis and seeking more purpose in life
>
> - Downshifting is a growing trend
>
> - A truly happy and successful life comes from finding and living out your unique purpose in life
>
> - Your life purpose is your unique reason for being, expressed through who you are and what you do
>
> - Different people find their purpose in different ways
>
> - You can find and live out your life purpose
>
> Now you've seen how you'll benefit from finding your life's purpose, the following chapters help you discover and equip you to pursue your purpose. You will gain new insights in relation to yourself, life, and your unique role here in this world.

o o o

STEP 1:
SEE LIFE AFRESH

GAIN A NEW PERSPECTIVE

○ ○ ○

STEP 1
See Life Afresh
Gain a New Perspective

○ ○ ○

*"Two men look out the same prison bars;
one sees mud, the other stars."*
(Beck Hansen – musician and songwriter)

○ ○ ○

The power of perspective

THE WAY YOU SEE LIFE affects how you feel and what you do. If you were to look out of prison bars would you see mud or would you see stars?

Your perception of life and the world around you has a huge impact. For example, if you believe the world to be an unsafe place you can feel scared and seek to protect yourself from harm by doing all you can to avoid dangerous situations. When it comes to planning a holiday you may choose to stay in your own country and only visit places you are familiar with and feel comfortable in. Contrary to that, your friends may see life differently and believe the world to be safe and full of new and exciting places to visit. So they go off on foreign holidays, avoiding the beaten track of popular tourist destinations, and come back with loads of photos and happy memories to share with you.

Your perspective is powerful; it controls how you behave. The world itself is as it is but your perception of it is the little thing that makes the big difference. There's a cause and effect process going on here. What you think affects how you feel, then your emotions influence your actions. But it all starts with what you think. And your thinking is

STEP 1: SEE LIFE AFRESH

based on your perspective, how you interpret life and the world around you to be.

So how have you come to develop your perspective? It's by a combination of nature and nurture; your natural inbuilt personality plus what you've experienced in life. There's been a lot of research done in this area. Some would say it's more down to your environment. If you've grown up in a supportive and loving family then you're more likely to feel confident, believing the world to be a good place. Others would argue against this and say it's more about your core character. They back this up with examples of people who've grown up in terrible circumstances yet remained hopeful and happy. Still others would say it's a choice. You can choose how you see life and what position you are going to take when forming your perspective.

My view is that it's a combination of all three. How you've been treated in life can have an impact. In my early career I worked for some unpleasant managers. There was one who could best be described as a child-like bully trapped in an adult's body. My view of the world of work was that it was an increasingly unpleasant place to be. Later on I found a job elsewhere with a fantastic manager and I remember saying to her, "Thank you for restoring my faith in employers." Then again, there are some who don't seem to change despite what's happening all around them. "Yes, that's Sally, the eternal optimist." And there are the others who seem to have had some kind of life-changing experience. "Have you seen Mohammed lately? I don't know what happened to him but it's like he's a different person!"

I'm convinced that it's possible to change your perspective. Taking the above example of choosing a holiday, you could decide to be brave and travel abroad to one of the less riskier places you've been reading about. Having spent a week or so there you may have to accept that no harm has come to you, the people have been friendly, and you've actually enjoyed yourself. The world now seems less dangerous than it was before. This may encourage you to be even more adventurous in future as your perspective changes. Within just a few years you may find yourself booking a holiday with your friends who are becoming increasingly excited about their plans to trek through the Andes!

The aim of this chapter is to help you gain a clearer perspective on life. I'm going to ask you to do a few exercises which, if you take them seriously, could totally transform the way you see your life. Gaining a clear perspective is the firm foundation on which you can build yourself a more fulfilling future.

Don't take life for granted

Joe was driving home when he realized something was wrong; he couldn't see the cars on the other side of the road – he was losing his sight. Arriving home he felt unwell; the sense of feeling in his fingers and toes left him and numbness was creeping over his body. Becoming confused, he struggled to speak. His memory was fading fast and he couldn't remember his wife's name. Rushed to the emergency admissions ward at the local hospital Joe was connected up to monitors as doctors tried to work out what was happening to him. Laying on the hospital bed in that emergency room, Joe realized these could be his last moments on earth. He didn't want to die; all he could do was pray. Joe was only 35.

How close are you to the end of your life? Is this something you've thought about recently, or do you try to push such an uncomfortable thought out of your mind? Benjamin Franklin, that great American politician once said, "In this world nothing is certain but death and taxes." With some effort you could evade the latter – but I've not met anyone yet who has escaped the former. Recognizing this fact can help to put your life into perspective. In the time it has taken you to read this short paragraph, it's estimated that another 50 people have closed their eyes and lost sight of this earth for the last time.

Joe was fortunate. The medical staff could give no explanation for what happened but he came through his ordeal. It took him a month

STEP 1: SEE LIFE AFRESH

to recover before he could return to work. He now realized he wasn't as indestructible as he first thought. Following that incident he learned to value each day far more than he had before. His wake-up call caused him to think seriously about what was most valuable to him — family, friends and doing something useful with his life.

If you've ever had a close encounter with death — either yours or someone else's — it's likely that you too will have reflected on how fragile life is. Valuing your time here on earth can help you to focus on those things that are more important. Choose to make the most of today. If you live every day as if it could be your last you're likely to get more out of life — and one day you'll be right. It's useful to bear in mind the words of Walter Payton, the American football legend, "Remember, tomorrow is promised to no one."

Several years ago I was leading a workshop helping people to make better use of their time and lives. As usual I asked delegates who they were and why they had attended. When one guy introduced himself the room fell silent. "Hi, I'm Mike. I'm 29 years old and have a wife and two kids. I've just been diagnosed with multiple sclerosis. The doctors told me I might have three years left before I'm confined to a wheelchair. I'm here to learn how I can make the best use of the next three years so I can provide for my family." Mike had learned an important lesson in life; value the time that you have while you still have time to value.

o o o o o o o o o o o o o o o o o o o o o o o o o o o o o o o o o o

EXERCISE: Your life's time-line
Draw a horizontal line in your notebook. This line represents your life with birth at the far left and death at the right. Mark on the line how far along you think you are in your journey.

o o o o o o o o o o o o o o o o o o o o o o o o o o o o o o o o o o

If you live in the developed world the average life expectancy is still around 70 years. If you are aged 35 you could place yourself roughly in the middle of the scale. However, if you were brought up in Africa, at age 35 you'd probably position yourself much closer to the right-hand side. Life expectancy in many parts of that vast continent still currently stands at around 40 years.

Happenstance and triggers

In one way the ancient Greek philosophy that encourages us to "live for today for tomorrow we die" makes some sense. Life is over far too soon. Therefore, we ought to enjoy it while we have it. Then again, in another way, it's too short-sighted. Sandra found this out the hard way. As a well-paid architect she enjoyed life and all its pleasures including meals out at her favorite restaurants with the odd glass (or two) of full-bodied red wine. Living in a picture-postcard cottage her commute to the job she loved took less than half an hour through countryside that looked beautiful at any time of year. She had more money than she needed and a great set of friends to enjoy her spare time with. Then one morning her manager asked Sandra to step into his office:

> *Sandra, I've got some bad news. You know our parent company has been struggling lately, well they're having to make some hard decisions. Our office is going to be closed down and there's no promise of any redeployment opportunities. We don't know the exact date yet but I'd guess we've got about a month left. This has come as a surprise to me also. As soon as I know more I'll let you know.*

Only minutes before she had felt on top of the world; now this same world had just come crashing down around her ears. The promised promotion she had so eagerly sought would now be no more. Worse than that, it was extremely unlikely she could find a similar job in her specialist field within a reasonable commuting distance. Without such well-paid work Sandra recognized that her idyllic cottage could be taken from her; the mortgage payments would soon exceed her reach. Three months would probably be the limit for survival with only a

STEP 1: SEE LIFE AFRESH

small redundancy package to fall back on. Suddenly, questions flooded her mind: "Why me? Why now? How will I survive? Where do I go from here?"

Creating and enjoying a happy lifestyle is a good thing to do. However, there is a risk with expecting it to continue forever; life happens and circumstances can change without warning – some call it "happenstance". If your happiness is based on the pleasures your current lifestyle provides and something happens to take them away you're likely to feel sad. Sometimes such changes can act as a trigger and cause you to question where you find real happiness in life.

When Sandra lost her job she started thinking. She didn't really want to leave the area but knew she couldn't afford to keep her lovely cottage without a well-paid job to cover the mortgage. Within three months she sold her house and moved into rented accommodation nearby. Because there were no other employers looking to recruit an architect, Sandra decided to start her own fledgling business serving local private customers. The work was a little different and presented a number of new challenges – but she is now adapting well. Her lifestyle is less extravagant than it used to be and the forced change caused her to re-evaluate her priorities.

At this stage Sandra doesn't know exactly what the future holds but she's more hopeful than she was. The experience has taught her that the happiness you can feel from living a comfortable, carefree lifestyle can evaporate quickly when hard times come. Working out what really matters to her and focussing more on these things now provides a deeper sense of inner satisfaction. Confronted by the harsh realities of life she has had time to stop, think and change her perspective.

Sometimes something happens in life that jolts you out of your normal routine and opens the door to a new way of seeing things. Joe saw things differently when he was staring up at the ceiling from a hospital bed. Sandra's unexpected redundancy pushed her into looking for a new way forward in life. When things happen that you don't expect you may find yourself asking questions such as, "What is this all about? Is this as good as it gets? And what on earth is the purpose of my life anyway?"

As difficult as it may be, I'd encourage you to try to welcome unexpected circumstances as friends, not reject them as intruders. They give us the opportunity to rethink life and the future. Common triggers for new ways of thinking include sudden illness or incapacity, the death of a loved one, redundancy, or a natural disaster nearby or elsewhere in the world. Such triggers jolt us out of our comfort and security and prompt us to think about the fragility and value of life.

Others may experience more pleasurable triggers such as watching a butterfly emerge from a cocoon, seeing a beautiful sunrise, hearing the lyrics of a song, smelling the scent of a particular fragrance or holding a newborn baby. Though these may appear less dramatic they can still be just as powerful as they inspire you to consider the wonder, complexity and beauty of life. Whether the experience is pleasant or painful, the opportunity to pause and look afresh at life should not be ignored.

EXERCISE: Life's triggers
What triggers have you experienced in life? How have you responded to them? How is your life different now as a result of them? Or have you forgotten the lesson you learned and slipped back into your previous way of living? Make a note of anything that you think is important as a result of asking yourself these questions.

Decide what's important

Mike was forced to face the facts, having been told he would soon be confined to a wheelchair he could see his active life on earth was limited. Because of that, he thought deeply about what was most important

STEP 1: SEE LIFE AFRESH

to him. For Mike, providing for his family was uppermost in his mind. Sandra too had to think. She wanted to stay living in the same area. Hopefully you're not faced with a situation to similar to that of Mike or Sandra. Having said that, even if you're not, it still pays to think seriously about what's important in life. Here's a simple exercise to get you thinking and help you focus in on what's most valuable to you. It should help you to appreciate the time that you have left and make better use of it.

○○○○○○○○○○○○○○○○○○○○○○○○○○○○○○○○○○○○○○

EXERCISE: Identifying what's most important
Imagine you've just visited your doctor and were told you only have 12 months to live. What would you want to do in the next year? (This could include jobs you want to finish, places you want to go, and people you want to spend time with.) List down your answers. How about if you only had three months? How does that change things?

○○○○○○○○○○○○○○○○○○○○○○○○○○○○○○○○○○○○○○

Having identified what's of primary importance to you, these are the things which you should focus your attention on. Everything else is secondary. Ask yourself how much time and effort are you giving to these things already. If they are so important, why wait until tomorrow to do something when you can make a start on them today? How will you feel if in a year's time you could look back at this list and see a tick next to each one because you've achieved all that you intended? Think about what you can do in the next week to give some time to these priorities. Record your thoughts in your notebook. We'll come back to the issue of working on your priorities later on.

Take time out to think

Oliver Wendell Holmes (the physician and poet) is on record as saying, "The mind, once expanded to the dimensions of larger ideas, never regains its original size." When you experience a trigger and allow a new and challenging thought to enter your mind it has an impact. You are then faced with a choice as to how to respond. One option is to consciously suppress the thought and push it back out of your mind, refusing to come to terms with it. More likely, you could allow the busyness and worries of life to take over and stifle it until you are deafened to its voice. Alternatively, you can give time to reflecting upon it and allow it to take root.

Like a garden plant, good thoughts benefit from careful cultivation. Just as plants need light, water and nutrients, you need to feed your thoughts for them to flourish and blossom. Through taking time out for personal reflection, applying a little natural curiosity and choosing to adopt a positive mental attitude, you can glean new insights that lead you forwards in your search for a more purposeful, happy and successful life. As well doing the exercises in this book, I'd encourage you to apply the same approach whenever you come across a useful thought or new insight. Capture it, dwell on it for a while, then set aside some time in future to come back and consider it again. This could be referred to as meditation.

One popular approach to meditation is to try to empty your mind of all thoughts. However, a much earlier understanding of the word meditation means "to ruminate upon a thought". Ruminate comes from the Latin word ruminare, literally "to chew the cud" as a cow would. Did you know cows have four different regions within their stomach? When they swallow grass it is initially held in the rumen part of the stomach. Later on they regurgitate the partially digested grass (or cud) to chew it over for a while before swallowing it again. This re-chewed grass then enters another part of the stomach where the cow's digestive system can extract more of the goodness and nutrients from it. Similarly, we can get more out of a thought if we capture it, bring it back to our attention later and chew over it for a while.

To meditate upon a thought you can ask yourself questions such as, "What does this mean for me? How might this impact my life if I was to fully take it on board? And what might I miss out on if I ignore or reject

STEP 1: SEE LIFE AFRESH

this thought?" Henry Ford has been quoted as saying, "Thinking is the hardest work there is, which is probably the reason so few engage in it." Within this book you will be challenged to do some of this hard work, stopping and thinking from time to time. I'd encourage you to capture your thoughts so you can come back to them later and chew them over from time to time. That way you can extract more value from them.

If you haven't already done so, I'd strongly recommend you find yourself a notebook or some other way of recording your thoughts in a place where you can quickly capture and easily retrieve them again. Also, see if you can pinpoint some times when you can pull your notebook out and go over your notes. If it helps, consider going away for a retreat for a day or more to be alone with your thoughts. Most people are unlikely to manage a whole day but why not find a quiet hour where you can withdraw to your favorite place such as your garden, or go for a stroll on the beach or a woodland walk? However you approach it, I know you will benefit from taking time out to think, meditate and ruminate.

Map your journey

Perhaps this is a good point to spend some more time in reflection. Building on the analogy of seeing life as a journey, you can benefit from thinking about what's happened along the way. An exercise that has helped many is to draw this out as a picture. The more time you give to this the more value you will gain from it.

○○○○○○○○○○○○○○○○○○○○○○○○○○○○○○○○○○○○○○

EXERCISE: Mapping out your life's journey

Follow the instructions below to map out your life's journey:

Go and find a blank sheet of paper, the larger the better. Now mark a point on the far left side and label it "birth". Close to the far right side mark another point "today". Starting at your point of birth draw a route from where you set off to where you are now. Think of your journey as a road you have travelled along in a car. On your journey you may have passed through quiet country lanes, busy congested cities, scenic routes or wide, quiet freeways. Your journey might have included intersections, roundabouts, bridges and tunnels. If you faced steep hills, pot-holes, one-way streets, stop signs, lay-bys or diversions, jot these down too. What was the weather like along the way; warm and sunny, wet and windy or dark and cold? Once you've drawn out your route label it describing what was happening along the way. Reflect on what you've drawn and answer the following:

1. What parts of the journey did you enjoy?
2. When did you feel most off-course?
3. Why was that and what does that tell you?
4. When did you know you were fully on-track and why was that?
5. What else can you learn as you think over your life in this way?

○ ○

Compare yourself to others

I know, you may have been brought up with parents who repeatedly told you to stop comparing yourself and your situation to others. "But Frank's parents bought him a brand new bicycle for his birthday!" "Yes darling, that might be so, but we can't afford a new bike. So stop comparing yourself to Frank." However, I'm going to ask you to do some comparing for a minute or two as this could affect your perspective on life.

It seems that comparing yourself to others is a natural tendency. The danger is we often compare ourselves to those who we believe are wealthier, happier and more successful than us. Again, we are often blinkered and look only at those living at the same time as us. Taking a broader view can provide a different perspective. Let's try thinking more widely, comparing ourselves to previous generations and other nations.

Throughout history people have become richer and acquired more possessions than their predecessors. Our current lifestyle would

STEP 1: SEE LIFE AFRESH

have been hard to envisage just two generations ago. In the developed world we are more affluent and can access a wider range of luxuries than has been possible for any other generation. However, this wealth is not evenly distributed. In 1906 the Italian economist and lecturer, Vilfredo Pareto, published a study showing that in his country 80 per cent of the land was owned by just 20 per cent of the people. The other 80 per cent of the population shared the remaining 20 per cent. Pareto's research indicated this uneven distribution of wealth was commonplace and is now widely known as the Pareto Principle – or the 80/20 rule. One century later, and applied globally, there is now an even greater polarization of wealth. According to a report by the World Institute for Development Economics Research at the United Nations University, the richest 10 per cent of adults possess 85 per cent of the world's total wealth. This is held primarily within North America, Europe and a few high-income Asian countries. Conversely, the poorer half of the world adult population owns only one per cent of global wealth.

If you have clothes to wear, enough food to eat, fresh water to drink, sanitation facilities and a place to shelter, you are still better off than an estimated 900 million people that the World Bank have identified as living in absolute poverty. While it seems that the rich are getting richer, there are still too many people living below the poverty line.

Edward DeBono came up with a three letter acronym to help us gain a fresh perspective. He said we should take into consideration OPV. These three letters stand for Other People's Viewpoint. If we could step outside of our own bodies and step into someone else's, what would the world look like through their eyes? What if you applied OPV to an 18th century factory worker at the beginning of the industrial revolution? How would you see life then? Or a 1st century fisherman in China? Or a 21st century subsistence farmer in Africa? Would you want to swop places with any of them?

When we compare ourselves with such people we may realize that actually we're pretty well off. By appreciating what we have rather than focusing on what we don't have but want, we can change our attitude and the feelings we experience. I've read more than once about doctors who have successfully treated patients afflicted with depression by giving them a very unusual prescription. They've been told to go home, look in the mirror and remind themselves out loud of all the good things they can be thankful for. Their health, their wealth, their friendships, and anything else that comes to mind. Doing this two or three times a day has yielded far better results than any tablets the doctor could have prescribed.

This idea isn't new though. It's been summed up in a 19th century spiritual song, "Count your blessings name them one by one." The idea is to shift your focus. See life from a higher and broader perspective. In doing so the dissatisfaction that may be troubling you will fade away and a greater sense of peace and happiness will descend upon you. The result? Instead of sinking into a lair of despair you will rise with an attitude of gratitude.

○○

EXERCISE: Count your blessings
Try the doctor's remedy. Ideally, wait until no-one else is around then look into a mirror and remind yourself out loud of all the good things you can be thankful for. Keep going for at least ten to fifteen minutes. If you're struggling to think of things then use OPV. See life from Other People's Viewpoints and appreciate how well off you are when you compare yourself to them. Notice your feelings before you start and after you finish.

○○

Take a shortcut – learn from others

You've got a choice. When it comes to learning about life, success and happiness you can choose trial and error and the school of hard knocks, or you can take a shortcut and learn from others. As you're reading this

STEP 1: SEE LIFE AFRESH

book I'm assuming you're open to learning from others. This way you'll progress more quickly and with less pain.

It's said that you remember the lessons you've been taught in life from your own mistakes far better that those of others you've seen. That may be true. There are plenty of things I've done in life which caused me pain in some shape or form which I can easily remember. However, life is too short to try to find the time to go out and make all the mistakes for yourself. Why bother? And why subject yourself to all that pain, frustration and regret anyway? Why not avoid as much of it as you can and speed up your learning process?

As well as learning from your own reflections, and from watching others, you can learn from people who have invested their lives into the study of your chosen subject. This way you can benefit from their wisdom and take a shortcut. When it comes to understanding happiness, becoming successful or finding your purpose in life there are plenty of people who've given time to thinking about this. We can learn from what they've discovered. Two areas people often turn to in their search for answers about the deeper things in life are philosophy and spirituality. So let's take a brief look at what they both have to offer.

Learn a lesson from philosophy

Firstly, philosophy, which incidentally means "the love of wisdom", encourages us to think about life from a logical point of view. Philosophers usually give their time to thinking about and discussing subjects such as existence, knowledge, truth, morality, ethics, and our relationship to the world around us. Two main schools of philosophical thought are the metaphysical and the ethical. Metaphysical philosophy tries to answer the questions: "What is real?" and, "How can I know?" Ethical philosophy takes a different approach and asks: "What is good?" Even a brief study of philosophy will reveal that different philosophers arrive at different conclusions. Trying to explain these varying points of view and relate them to everyday life is a major task in itself and well beyond the scope of this book. However, without trying to appear too simplistic, there are two conclusions most philosophers would agree upon:

1. We should take life seriously and think about it

2. If we're alive, we should try to do good

As you've reached this far in this book I'm sure you're taking a serious approach to life. When it comes to doing good, you'll explore that in more depth in the next step when you'll clarify what you believe is worthwhile from your perspective on life. Thinking is good; action as a result of thinking is better.

Get a revelation from spirituality

Wait! Before you close this book thinking I'm going to get all religious on you, I'm not. I firmly believe that we can learn something from any philosophy, every faith and each individual. Some of the people I've met while preparing this book have a faith but many don't. Having said that, let's take a brief look at what we can learn from spirituality.

Whereas philosophy relies upon logic in an attempt to find answers to some basic questions, spirituality encourages us to seek insights from beyond the realm of human reasoning alone. It moves the focus from the physical to the spiritual. Spirituality encompasses both traditional religion and alternative belief systems.

In his book on *The World's Living Religions*, theologian and teacher Robert Hume refers to religion as "the common characteristic of mankind". History records that all over the world in every significant culture people have believed in something or someone greater than themselves. This has implications for anyone with a faith reading this book; they must consider the meaning and purpose of life from within the context of their own spiritual point of view.

STEP 1: SEE LIFE AFRESH

Paul Tillich, a German philosopher and theologian, came to a challenging conclusion: "Being religious means asking passionately the question of the meaning of our existence and being willing to receive answers, even if the answers hurt." It's possible that if you seriously question the purpose of your life you may begin a journey of enquiry that leads you to an unexpected destination. Honest enquiry means being willing to take that risk. To not explore certain paths of thought keeps a door closed behind which there may be an answer for your life. Many people, frightened of what they may find, choose to never open that door. Others persist with a fixed view of spirituality based on their upbringing or what they've heard others say without honestly exploring it for themselves. If you feel uncomfortable thinking about such things I'd encourage you to ask yourself why. You might start with the question, "What if something within spirituality holds part of the answer for me?"

Without going into great depth, it might be worth summarising a few insights that can be gleaned from popular religious beliefs. First, there are those that believe in many gods, some who claim there can logically only be one divine being, and a few that talk more about a "universal consciousness" rather than a god. All faiths imply we are subservient to a higher power. Within many religions there are devoted followers who claim you can have a tangible spiritual experience or a personal encounter with God. Such believers are more passionate about their faith viewing God as a present reality who takes an ongoing interest in their lives. With such a belief comes the expectation of some form of two-way relationship. This relationship can provide ongoing guidance that is helped through prayer, meditation or reflection on inspirational or sacred writings. These sacred writings are assumed to have authority when it comes to defining the meaning and purpose of a life and also provide some guidance on how to live. More than half the population of the world claims to have some allegiance to an established religion. The following summarizes the main beliefs of the world's most popular religions in relation to the purpose of life:

Religion	Followers	Purpose
Christianity	2 billion	Love God, love others
Islam	1.3 billion	Submit to the will of God
Hinduism	900 million	Escape the bonds that tie us to illusions and continual rebirth
Buddhism	360 million	Avoid suffering, gain enlightenment and release from rebirth
Sikhism	23 million	Overcome self, align with the will of God
Taoism	20 million	Seek peace and inner harmony
Judaism	14 million	Keep God's commandments
Confucianism	6 million	Serve society honourably
Baha'i	6 million	Develop spirituality and draw close to God
New Age	5 million	Create your own spiritual belief system

Religion ultimately suggests that if God exists then it's worth making the effort to find out about him/her/it and to live within that faith's guidelines. Atheists can ignore the above as they don't believe there is a God; agnostics can remain open-minded and learn from the above without being sure whether God exists or not.

When it comes to spirituality there are three approaches you can take: follow the lead offered by your family or community; choose one that fits best with what you currently believe; or do some thorough research and conclude which one makes most sense to you. I started with a pick'n'mix New Age approach, choosing elements from a number of faiths to suit myself. After some time I uncovered inconsistencies within my combined belief system so I started some more thorough research. This led to a clear conclusion and a personal choice. Ultimately, your

STEP 1: SEE LIFE AFRESH

beliefs about religion and spirituality will have some bearing on how you see life and your purpose within it.

Having said all this, a spiritual belief by itself might still not provide the full answer to the question about your individual life purpose. I've met many people who have a strong faith but are uncertain about what to give their time and energies to. Spirituality can offer you some general guidelines but it could still be up to you to decide exactly what to do with your life.

ooooooooooooooooooooooooooooooooooooooo

EXERCISE: Thinking about spirituality
What role has spirituality played in your life? Have you sought or received spiritual guidance before? How has it shaped your decision-making? Have you pondered the possibility of the existence of God? Capture your thoughts on spirituality before you move on.

ooooooooooooooooooooooooooooooooooooooo

Do you have a destiny?

Some people believe that every part of life is predestined. The motto attached to life could be summed up in the lyrics of the old Doris Day song, "Que sera, sera. Whatever will be, will be." Some think your future is set and based on the date of your birth, possibly linked to the position of the stars at that time. Others in some religions hold the view that God (or the gods) already has your future mapped out for you and your life is like that of a pawn being moved around by an unseen hand in a giant game of chess. With a belief such as this your job is to look outwards and yield to the forces that be so you can get yourself in line with what's been planned for you.

A related idea, but one that is less controlling, is to see your life as having been planned for in advance and captured within a blueprint hidden deep inside of yourself. Just like your fingerprints or your DNA, your purpose in life is unique and encoded within the very core of your being. If this is so, your responsibility is to look inside to uncover this hidden plan and then choose to live it out.

The concept of prophecy seems to support the theory of predestination. Nostradamus, the Mayans, fortune-tellers and people of many faiths have made predictions about the future. Many seem to come true; some don't. Perhaps the greatest concentration of fulfilled prophecy centres on the life of Jesus Christ. According to the Wycliffe Bible Encyclopaedia, the mathematical probability that Jesus could fulfil all the prophecies written about him in his 33 years is "one chance in 84 followed by 98 zeros". In other words, we can say it was statistically impossible for the prophets to predict what would happen and for Jesus to fulfil such prophecies by chance. It seems he was predestined to live the life he did – foretold by people who lived hundreds and thousands of years beforehand.

In contrast to predestination, an alternative viewpoint says you are free to do what you want and the future is entirely in your hands. Your decisions today could change world events and the lives of millions. If there is no God, or if the gods take a hands-off approach, you are the designer of your own destiny. The logical conclusion of this is that you must choose to take responsibility for your own actions and future. This doesn't mean you are completely free to do what you want as others around will remind you that "no man is an island". You will still be expected to conform to society's norms, something you will quickly discover if you try to live outside of the legal or tax systems. You may desire to be free – but the rest of society will only allow you to live freely within the constraints it places around you.

Even in traditional faiths such as Christianity there are some who hold differing views. At one end of the spectrum there are the extreme Calvinists who would say your life is predestined and your future is already decided. At the other end are the Armenians who counter that by saying you have a free will and can choose your future, (though

STEP 1: SEE LIFE AFRESH

paradoxically they still suggest God is in control and he already knows the future). Each would try to convince you that how you get to that future is different.

If you've ever struggled with the tension between destiny and choice without reaching a conclusion, could I suggest a third option which avoids the two extremes? I was once challenged by someone older and wiser than I with the question, "Do you see life as a tightrope or a highway?" Until that time I had viewed life as a tightrope; I had to strive hard to keep my balance, fearing the consequences of falling from my precarious position. The question immediately challenged my thinking but it took several months before it fully sunk in.

If you see life as a tightrope you will live with constant tension. You will always be looking for guidance to confirm that you're still on the rope. Where you find that guidance will vary depending on your belief system – perhaps in sacred writings, astrology, or the words of a religious figure or guru. The more concerned you are to stay on the tightrope, the more time (and sometimes money) you invest in seeking guidance. I know, I've been there.

Choosing to see life as a highway provides you with direction, boundaries, a choice of speeds to travel at, and even the opportunity to take detours and get back on track later. I'd suggest seeing life as a highway because it gives you more flexibility and takes away the fear that you'll miss the way. If you reach a point where you feel you're off-track you can always head back for the highway and adjust your speed if you want to. There are consequences with the highway approach though: you still need to take responsibility for your own future, the direction you will follow, how close you come to the boundaries and the pace you will travel at.

ooooooooooooooooooooooooooooooooooooooo

EXERCISE: Destiny and choice
Look back over your life until now and think about this issue of choice and destiny. Choose the statement that most applies to you:

1. *"I've been wandering aimlessly."*
2. *"I've been trying to walk a tightrope."*
3. *"I've been travelling a multi-lane highway."*

o o o o o o o o o o o o o o o o o o o o o o o o o o o o o o o o o o o o

This exercise might appear simple on the surface but it's really important to get right. If you've been wandering aimlessly or trying to walk a tightrope, choosing to take a highway approach is like arriving at a major intersection in your life. You can change the way you are heading. In doing so you will benefit as you take greater responsibility for your future. If you've been wandering aimlessly you will gain more focus; if you've been struggling to stay balanced on your tightrope you will feel a sense of liberation.

Recognize your potential

You've probably met people with over-inflated egos who think they are the centre of the universe. You may have also met others whose self-esteem is so low they talk of themselves as if they have nothing to offer this world. Both of them need help – but in different ways.

Jane suffered from a lack of confidence. She struggled at school and was labelled as "educationally subnormal". As she grew up people weren't nice to her and she found life very hard. On several occasions she tried to take her own life – but failed. "I couldn't even do that properly" she told me. Later in life she married, had children and a couple of part-time jobs. Work was difficult for Jane. She confided that she never really felt part of the team: "I'm not like normal people, you know." Along the way she found a religious faith that helped give life a clearer perspective, but she still struggled to recognize her worth. Then she found a job supporting children with special educational needs. "It's kind of odd you know, but I can relate to these kids. They trust me and I understand how they feel." When she talks about these children and how she helps them

STEP 1: SEE LIFE AFRESH

with their struggles her eyes light up. It seems their behaviour in class has been improving and Jane has won a place in their hearts. It might have taken her nearly 50 years, but Jane has found her life has purpose as she brightens up the lives of others. And it's made her happier too.

Sometimes people start to do something they believe in without recognizing the longer-term potential. Born in Albania in 1910, Agnes Gonxha Bojaxhiu wanted to help children poorer than her. Aged 19 she went to teach in a missionary schoolhouse in India. As the years passed and she took on more responsibility, she broadened the range of support she and her friends offered to those around her. Having quietly served others for nearly 70 years she left a legacy that helped create 610 missions in 123 countries and has inspired millions. We remember her as Mother Teresa of Calcutta.

Consider the impact that two young Americans have had on so many of us. In their mid-twenties Larry Page and Sergey Brin set up a new company to "organize the world's information and make it universally accessible and useful". By mid-2012, just 14 years later, they've built up a business that currently employs about 55,000 staff and probably uses about two million computers that handle more than a billion requests for information every day. The company name if you haven't already guessed it is Google, the world's most successful internet search engine.

Then there are people like the Scottish biologist Alexander Fleming who experimented with moulds and discovered the modern wonder drug, penicillin; American inventor Thomas Edison who developed the first useable light bulb; and the Wright brothers who loved to play with machinery and created the first successful "heavier than air" flying machine.

Could any of them have really known what impact they would have on the rest of the world? Similarly, neither can you. It doesn't matter if you discover your calling early in life like Mother Teresa or later like Jane, whether you touch the lives of millions or just a few, the fact remains: your life has potential.

Live for the future (but in the present)

Already you've been encouraged to reflect on the past and think a bit about the future. I'm wondering, what do you think about most: the past, the present or the future? Do you find yourself regularly talking about the good old days when you were younger? Alternatively, do you spend time daydreaming and thinking about what life might be like years from now? Perhaps you are like Peter who I've discovered lives very much in the present. He's so excited by what is happening around him every day he doesn't have much time for anything else. When with his children he joins in with whatever they're doing. He doesn't reminisce too much and when I raised the matter of long-term planning and goal-setting he looked at me quizzically and asked, "Do I need to do that?" Peter lives very much in the present.

Living continually in the past can cause problems for you. Judith Leary-Joyce, author of *The Psychology of Success* explains why:

> *For some, this time of inspiration comes just once in their lives – they have one major peak, then keep trying to repeat it rather than moving on. Their energy begins to stagnate and all they can do is look back. The episode where they lived day by day with their passion becomes 'the best years of my life' because nothing before or since has ever matched up. This is the recipe for years of regret, knowing there is more and not being able to access it.*

The past is important but you shouldn't imprison yourself by it. Reflect on it, learn from it, then apply those lessons within the present. Similarly, there's a danger that comes from trying to live forever in the future. Hoping for better days ahead, talking about what to do next year and planning how to spend your retirement can be exciting. However, dreams can remain just that – dreams – unless you take action in the present to turn them into reality.

If you're looking for a clearer sense of purpose, more happiness, or greater success in life, what you're saying is you want the future to be better than today. Sometimes it's the disappointments with the past that push us to change things in the present so we can create a better future. So there is a need to focus on the future but it's equally important to do something now. Procrastination is the art of putting off until tomorrow something you could benefit from were you to take action today. That's why in this book I encourage you to capture your thoughts as you have them and to take action as soon as you can. Why put off starting something new until tomorrow when you can begin today? You will feel better for it knowing you are now one step closer to your goal. When you get a fresh insight or come up with a new plan ask yourself, "What one action can I take today to apply this in a practical way and move me forward towards my goal?"

You can learn from the past, you can plan for the future, but you need to take action in the present. To find your purpose, become happier, and live a successful life, you need to do all three.

Become more purposeful

In the introduction we saw that some people find their purpose quickly and easily while others discover it with the passing of time. The exercises in this book may trigger a sudden revelation. Alternatively, they could offer a type of scaffolding within which you construct your own future. If finding and living your life purpose takes you longer to achieve than it does for others, don't worry, I'm sure you'll find it easier the more you work at it.

Some people start out unclear as to what it's all about. They may feel they are drifting and purposeless. If that's you then your next step is to focus on something you feel is more worthwhile to help you shift from purposeless to more purposeful. As you work at those things which are more purposeful you will gain greater clarity and are more likely to settle on something which you feel is much closer to your unique purpose in life.

If you're at the stage where you find it hard to visualize a specific purpose for your life then don't panic. Perhaps you might find it helpful to ask yourself the question, "What would make my life more purposeful?" By doing this you will be making progress in the right direction. I'm told it's easier to steer a moving ship. What that means is that if you are making an effort and trying out something you are moving forward. As you go on you will get a clearer sense of whether it's working for you or not. Your inner guidance system (which we'll talk more about later) will tell you if you are on track or off course. This feedback will help you judge whether you need to change direction or not. Choosing to live more purposefully and taking action today could be the first step in your journey of discovery. If you persist, I'm sure that in the end you will hit upon something so special that you'll realize that at last you've found your unique purpose in life.

EXERCISE: Becoming more purposeful
On a scale of 1 to 10, (1 being low and 10 being high), how purposeful would you say your life is right now? Why is that? What could you do to increase your score and sense of purposefulness?

Key thoughts to take away:

This chapter has been about putting your life into context and gaining a fresh perspective. Recognizing your days on earth are limited should help you resolve to make best use of the time you have left. Life should be fun but it's not a game to be played too casually. Here are some key thoughts for you to take away from this chapter:

STEP 1: SEE LIFE AFRESH

- You can choose a different perspective
- Recognizing how far along you are in life's journey helps bring things into focus
- Life happens so pay attention to life's trigger events
- It's important to decide what's important
- Take time out to think
- Philosophy, religion and spirituality all offer some useful thoughts on the meaning and purpose of life
- Seeing life as a highway can give you a sense of direction without being too constrictive
- Your life has potential
- Learn lessons from the past, consider the future, but take action in the present
- Choosing to live more purposefully can lead you to your unique life purpose

With the benefit of a clearer perspective, you're now ready for the next step. The following chapter will guide you to think through what's really worth doing while you're here on planet earth. Clarifying this is a major stepping-stone on your journey to living a happy and successful life.

o o o

STEP 2:
DO SOMETHING WORTHWHILE

WORK OUT WHAT'S IMPORTANT TO YOU

○ ○ ○

STEP 2
Do Something Worthwhile
Work Out What's Important to You

○ ○ ○

"I want to leave this Earth just knowing that I've tried to give something back and tried to do something worthwhile with myself."
(Patrick Swayze – American actor)

○ ○ ○

See the bigger picture

MANY YEARS AGO I WAS PROVIDING some management training for a group of team leaders in a factory that made glass tubes. I've got to admit, the thought of working at a machine making glass tubes all day long didn't excite me. Looking around though, the staff seemed generally happy and engrossed in their work. One of the subjects we covered in the training programme was staff motivation. As part of the course I had to teach them about Maslow's Hierarchy of Needs; McGregor's Theory X and Theory Y Management and also Herzberg's Hygiene Factors and Motivators. While each of these theories had something useful to say about staff motivation, my intuition told me that when it came to keeping these workers happy and focused I was missing something. What was it that kept this place buzzing as they made glass tube after glass tube? Then one of the team leaders drew my attention to a poster on the wall:

See these tubes Mervyn, these aren't just any old glass tubes. What we're making here are high precision components used for a very special purpose.

STEP 2: DO SOMETHING WORTHWHILE

Did you know we're the only company in the world that makes these particular tubes? We're very proud of them. Do you know what they're used for? Look here's one in this picture...

Sure enough, right there on the poster you could see one of their tubes. It was an essential part of a life-support machine designed specifically for premature babies. Just like the rest of the staff in that factory I then got it. Their work wasn't about making glass tubes; it was about saving the lives of young children. They taught me a lesson that day. I found the hidden factor that kept the staff motivated. It was simply that they recognized how valuable and worthwhile their work really was.

Getting a fresh perspective on your work can change the way you feel about it. Being able to see that what you do is worthwhile is one of the three secrets of success in work that Ken Blanchard talks about in his book *Gung Ho!* He refers to it as having "the spirit of the squirrel". You see, squirrels could choose to laze around in the treetops and enjoy the warmth of the summer sun – but they don't. Instead, they busy themselves gathering and storing up nuts. Why? Because somehow they know that nuts are plentiful in summer but scarce in winter. They recognize that their hard work is worthwhile. That's why they keep at it.

Here are three approaches you could take to help you recognize ways in which your work may be both valuable and worthwhile:

1. Work is a means to an end: worth comes mainly from knowing you can support the needs of yourself and your family from the income you earn. To provide for yourself and those you love is a natural instinct. Knowing you can do so brings a sense of inner fulfilment.

2. Work is more about those you work with than what you do: worth can be found in developing meaningful relationships with those you have contact with on a day-to-day basis. The time you invest in colleagues, customers, members of the public, patients or others can

become the focus of your attention. People you relate to are more important than products you sell or tasks you complete.

3. Work fulfils a purpose for others: worth comes from seeing the practical benefits that others get from your efforts. Being able to show the direct link between your work output and the improvement in someone else's life can be immensely satisfying. You are making the world a better place

If your work meets all three of the above criteria then you can congratulate yourself on finding a worthwhile role. However, getting a fresh insight and seeing how it meets just one of these can help transform a frustrating job into one that's more fulfilling.

○○○○○○○○○○○○○○○○○○○○○○○○○○○○○○○○○○○○

EXERCISE: Seeing the bigger picture
Think about what you give your time to. Where do you see the value? In what way is it worthwhile? Are you supporting yourself and your loved ones? Are you brightening up the lives of other people? Are you making the world a better place? Or do you feel you could be doing something more worthwhile than what you're currently doing? Capture your thoughts in your notebook or file.

○○○○○○○○○○○○○○○○○○○○○○○○○○○○○○○○○○○○

Decide what's worthwhile

Different people have different ideas as to what's worthwhile in life. That's a good thing. If we all left our current homes to go off and serve the destitute and dying in India like Mother Teresa did, that country would suddenly become overcrowded and we'd add to any problems they already had. Helping the poor on the other side of the world is worthwhile, but so is helping people who live closer to home. You don't have to get on a plane or even a bus to find someone who would

STEP 2: DO SOMETHING WORTHWHILE

benefit from your support and help. There are people living nearby who are elderly, infirm or struggling with life that would really welcome just a little bit of help. Tidying their garden, fetching some shopping or just popping in for a chat can make a big difference to their lives.

But doing something worthwhile isn't just about focusing on people. You don't have to give up your whole life and become a missionary before you can claim that what you're doing is worthwhile. There are plenty of other things you can do. What you believe to be worthwhile depends upon your personal values (something we'll explore further in a later chapter) and your current circumstances. At this stage, just think about what you believe is worthwhile, even if it doesn't directly benefit anyone else.

Ken Jones and his wife lived near the coast. One winter's day in 1958 he came across a newly born seal pup washed up on the beach. After taking it home and nursing it back to health word got around that this was something Ken was good at. Over the next few years he took in and cared for an increasing number of injured seals and oiled birds, returning them to the wild as soon as they were ready. By 1975 Ken's small garden could no longer cope with the growing number of requests for help so he found a patch of land where he gradually built a range of pools for the seals. Because some would never be fit enough to survive life out in their natural environment, Ken allowed them to stay at his sanctuary as long-term guests. Since then the sanctuary has developed an animal hospital on site and has become a public attraction where people pay to visit. This has helped to fund the ongoing work that has also seen them care for dolphins, turtles, sea lions and penguins. As the seal sanctuary has grown, so has the team of helpers who also enjoy caring for these animals and nursing them back to full health. This is truly a worthwhile cause.

Tim Smit loved working with plants. He helped restore The Lost Gardens of Heligan, which has become one of the most visited gardens of Cornwall. While doing this he came up with an idea of creating a different type of garden. Taking a disused quarry, with the help of funders and a team of equally passionate people, he created The Eden Project based around two huge biomes, one replicating a tropical environment, the other a Mediterranean setting. Since opening in 2001, more than 12 million people have visited the site to enjoy being immersed in a carefully maintained ecosystem that houses around one million plants. But it's much more than just a garden, it's an educational charity. The Eden Project regularly works with schools, colleges, businesses and other communities to help raise awareness about environmental issues. They've also branched out and support a wide range of other projects including setting up vegetable gardens for school-children in Africa and low-carbon cooking stoves for rural families in Cambodia. Though Sir Tim wouldn't take all the credit himself, as a result of this one man and his passion for plants, millions have gained a greater awareness of the environment and been challenged to think about living a more sustainable and eco-friendly lifestyle.

Which of the above do you feel you can relate to best? Could you see yourself joining The Eden Project or a similar organization in an effort to protect the natural world around us? Or how about helping care for injured animals in a seal or donkey sanctuary? Or would a role where you're doing something that more directly benefits people suit you better? If this has sparked any new thoughts in your mind, it could be worth capturing them now.

Find a cause that's bigger than yourself

If you're focused purely on making life better for yourself then the only person you're likely to recruit to your cause is the one you can see in the mirror. As a contrast, by choosing to do something that's going to help make the world a better place you'll be creating a vision that the wider community will buy into. There are probably now well in excess of two million different charities in the world. America alone has more than

STEP 2: DO SOMETHING WORTHWHILE

1.2 million registered with the Internal Revenue Service. Each one was started with the aim of doing something worthwhile and with the hope that others would be attracted and want to give their support.

In recent years there has been a huge growth in organizations known as social enterprises. These are commercially viable businesses set up with the aim of giving back in some way. Unlike private businesses that have the aim of maximising profit, their focus is on doing something of worth for a specific community they serve. This could be to help people living locally, or to support others further afield. Examples of well-known UK-based social enterprises include The Big Issue, The Eden Project, Jamie Oliver's Fifteen restaurant and Cafedirect. Each of these has a clearly stated social mission explaining how they hope to achieve a beneficial environmental or social outcome. Some social enterprises attract grants but primarily they are self-sustaining through selling goods or services. A survey conducted by the Royal Bank of Scotland in 2011 found that while income generated by the largest FTSE100 businesses grew by 5% and small private business increased by 9%, social enterprise income leapfrogged them both growing by 14%. But as we've said, it's not just about the money. Through the efforts of social enterprises during this time the lives of millions were improved. Unemployed people have been helped to find work; fledgling start-up businesses were provided with workspace and other facilities; books, clothes and furniture have been recycled; Fairtrade farmers have found new markets; hungry people were fed; plus much, much more.

One other area that shouldn't be overlooked is the public sector. Over the years I've worked alongside, trained and coached many people who have been employed as public servants. This has included teachers who want to educate children, hospital staff dedicated to nursing patients, regeneration workers who focus on improving local communities and many more. I've found such people are usually motivated towards doing something purposeful in society. One guy I remember meeting had a passion for trees. He found a job where he went out looking at trees in the county where he lived. His role was to assess their condition and make recommendations for how keep them safe and healthy so they didn't fall down and cause trouble for others. What struck me was his infectious enthusiasm for his work and the fact that he was being paid to spend all day doing what he loved.

One of the benefits of getting involved in a charity, a social enterprise or the public sector is that you can feel you're part of something larger. The cause is bigger than just you and you can be reassured that what you're doing is helping to make the world a better place. Choosing a cause that is greater than yourself usually gives you something to work at for many years, if not the rest of your life. Additionally, you have a choice: you can work as a volunteer, or a paid employee, or you can take responsibility for setting up and running an enterprise yourself. You could approach your role by working full-time, part-time, or on an occasional basis. I'd recommend pausing to think about this for a moment.

○○○

EXERCISE: 50 worthwhile causes
Set aside at least 15 minutes, preferably more. Now make a list of 50 causes that are bigger than yourself. You'll probably find it easy to identify 10, 20 or even 30. However, once you've exhausted the easily recognized ones you have to think more carefully to come up with new ideas. Look back over your list. Do you notice common patterns? Are there any you feel particularly drawn to or moved by? Could these be worthwhile causes you might like to investigate further?

○○○

Support someone else's cause

You don't have to create your own cause; you can join with others who are already doing something worthwhile. When I was younger, one of my cousins got involved in the Save the Whale pressure group.

STEP 2: DO SOMETHING WORTHWHILE

At the same time, a good friend joined the Campaign for Nuclear Disarmament. If they had acted alone it would have been unlikely that anyone would have taken notice of them. As they joined with others who were equally as passionate as they were they became a force to be reckoned with. Sometimes it's only when enough people come together and focus on the same goal that they create a critical mass that makes things happen.

It's perfectly okay to be one of the crowd. In fact, it's often easier to work towards a goal when you've got the encouragement of others around you. One of the dangers that you can face when working alone is the tendency to give up when things get difficult. When you're part of a team this is far less likely to happen. If you're feeling a bit down one day then talking to a friend who's also focused on the same things as you are can help to lift you up again. And when you get the chance to encourage others in your group it will give you a boost too. You're also likely to learn new things from those around you who are further along the path than you are.

If you're uncertain as to what to do, just doing something is usually better than doing nothing. Rather than sitting at home and letting life pass you by why not get out and find something worthwhile to do? I remember a woman who had time on her hands and enjoyed being in the countryside. She joined a conservation volunteer group and met plenty of interesting people. She also learned new skills as she made paths through woodlands, built stone walls, cleared overgrown hedgerows and did many other things. As well as having a good time when she was out there volunteering, she could go back later and still get a sense of satisfaction from seeing what the team had accomplished together. Several years later she was given a new opportunity and trained to become a volunteer in a hospital chaplaincy team. Her focus shifted from improving the countryside to bringing comfort to those who were suffering. Both roles were worthwhile, both were supporting someone else's vision and both provided a sense of satisfaction, but without starting out as a conservation volunteer it's possible she may never have become a trained member of a chaplaincy team.

∘∘

EXERCISE: Supporting someone else's cause
Take a moment to think. Which would you prefer, blazing a trail by yourself or joining with others to support a shared cause? If you prefer to team up with others, what type of causes appeal to you? Are there others you know who have a passion for something that you also feel drawn towards?

∘∘

Giving to worthwhile causes

One way to support worthwhile causes is with your time and energies. Another way is to give money. There are charitable causes who refer to those who make donations as partners. There's a good reason for this. Such charities recognize that those who give financially are just as important as those who are on the front line serving. It's a partnership arrangement and without the givers there would be no resource available for the doers. They need each other. If you've ever given to charity then please recognize that your donations have helped changed lives for the better.

You may be drawn to specific causes. When our children were younger, one of our daughters had an interest in animals. When it came to donating clothes and toys that the children had grown out of we chose to give to a local animal welfare charity. Several years later, after my wife's grandmother died of cancer, we chose to divert this type of giving to the local Cancer Research charity shop. We've also given to other causes such as helping to buy livestock, farming equipment and food for people in Africa; hand-operated sewing machines for women in India; Christmas shoe boxes for children in Eastern Europe; and others. You're likely to find that different causes appeal to you at different times of life. Sometimes you can give money, sometimes you give unwanted

STEP 2: DO SOMETHING WORTHWHILE

goods that charities can turn into money. Don't underestimate your giving just because you're not there seeing the end result.

Occasionally I've met individuals who have criticized wealthy people, especially those who've made a lot of money through business. It seems they resent others who have more than they have. Sometimes I think they do this out of envy, wishing they too could be just as rich. There are two things I've learnt from years of studying people who have succeeded in business. The first is that generally they've worked very hard to get what they've got. The second is that very often these wealthy people give much more to charity than the rest of us do. Take Bill Gates as an example. Through developing Microsoft he's provided employment for thousands of people and given us software that has made work and learning so much easier and faster. Having more money than they need, Bill and his wife Miranda have set up a Foundation that has currently given away more than 25 billion dollars to worthwhile causes. Then there's Warren Buffet, the famous investor, who has personally pledged to give 99% of his 44 billion dollar estate to good causes. Coming together, the three of them have launched The Giving Pledge where they are encouraging others to give away the majority of their wealth to philanthropy. So far they have recruited more than 90 billionaires including Facebook founder Mark Zuckerberg, film-writer George Lucas and media mogul Ted Turner. In an open letter commenting on his philanthropic giving, Mr Turner wrote:

> *I don't measure success in numbers, but I consider my contributions of more than 1.3 billion dollars to various causes over the years to be one of my proudest accomplishments and the best investment I've ever made. Those dollars have improved lives, saved species, fought disease, educated children, inspired change, challenged ideas and opened minds; and at the time of my death, virtually all of my wealth will have gone to charity. Looking back, if I had to live my life over, there are things I would do differently, but the one thing I would not change is my charitable giving.*

Have you ever thought about making charitable donations? It's been said that if you can give your money away you own it; if you can't give it away it owns you. In your own life, who has more power, you or your money?

As well as giving to a good cause while you're alive, you can also give following your death. Including a charitable donation in your will can make a difference to others long after you've gone. Most charities have people who can help you with this.

It's true that you won't be able to meet the needs of everyone in the world tomorrow, but, you could start to make a difference in the life of someone today. Without the generosity of others, many charities would cease to exist overnight. Giving to those who are less fortunate than ourselves can also remind us how wealthy we are and helps put life back into perspective. If there are any actions you want to follow through on in relation to this jot your thoughts down in your notebook. This next exercise encourages you to think about what you can use money for apart from meeting your own needs.

ooooooooooooooooooooooooooooooooooooooooo

EXERCISE: Giving to a worthwhile cause
Imagine you made it onto the rich list and had more money than you could easily spend. What else could you do with your surplus cash? In answering this question you might identify some worthwhile causes that deserve further investigation. Again, record your answers in your notebook.

ooooooooooooooooooooooooooooooooooooooooo

Finding purpose in everyday life

Some of the examples we've just been talking about sit at the extreme end of the spectrum. Most of us are unlikely to make so much money that we will be approached personally and asked to join The Giving Pledge. Those signing up to join missionary organizations are also in

STEP 2: DO SOMETHING WORTHWHILE

the minority. It may be impractical for you to give up your job to head off into the Amazon jungle to try to save it by yourself. Not everyone wants to completely change the world around them. In fact, if they did, life on earth would probably be in total chaos.

There are many who prefer the stability of a normal life and see their primary purpose as providing and caring for their immediate family. Paul, a friend of mine, works for the local council as a Play Coordinator. He's passionate about his job and seeks to make sure that all children's public play areas are a safe place to be. He's found purpose in his everyday employment and the income it provides supports his growing family. Seeing him at peace within his own skin, I have the greatest respect for him.

Many women find themselves in a role where they devote most of their time to caring for their partner and children. Though not widely appreciated, this is still work – very hard work at times. You might not be paid for your labour but what you do is still essential. Without your continued efforts your family would suffer. In modern society the role of homemaker is often overlooked and undervalued. Last year I met a young woman who has happily chosen to be home-educated. Now in her late teens, she has worked closely with her mother to learn a variety of skills including cooking, caring for younger children and maintaining a clean and tidy home. When I asked her how she saw the future unfolding she told me her aim was to be a good wife and mother. To meet a young woman with an attitude such as this seems quite unusual in the modern society and many would label it as being "old-fashioned". I feel sure that when she marries, her future spouse will find they have a mature woman who has already embraced her purpose as a wife, mother and an accomplished homemaker.

In many cases the man is the major breadwinner while the woman looks after the family. However, there are times when the role is reversed. Shortly after getting married, Gary and Katie chose to start a family. Katie had the better-paid job, one that she enjoyed. Gary on the other hand was ready for a change. After some deliberation, they took the decision for Gary to become the main carer releasing Katie to return to work and provide financially for the family. Sure, Gary admits the role reversal was a bit of a challenge at times – but they found a way to make it work. Being a stay-at-home dad did have its benefits, probably the greatest was the strength of relationships he was able to form with his growing children. Gary recognized that his main purpose in life while the children were small was to hold the home together and make sure the children were well cared for.

Society around us consciously or unconsciously seeks to condition us. Fame and fortune are valued; an ordinary life can be despised. But is this really right? Rob Parsons, author of *The Sixty Minute Father* and coach to many wealthy and successful business-people has said, "I've never met anyone who at the end of their life said they wished they spent more time at the office." At that stage in life when time runs out you realize more pointedly what is most worthwhile and valuable in life – and it's not money and what it can buy. Loving and nurturing your family is more important than creating wealth. Roger and Rebecca Merrill, writers of *Life Matters*, emphasize that "family is the fundamental principle of personal happiness and of a regenerating, renewing society. The most important 'success' is success at home, and making each generation better is the way we best contribute to society as a whole." If you have responsibility for nurturing children then be encouraged by Dr Phil McGraw. In *Family Matters* he states that, "Your role as a parent is the highest, noblest calling you will ever have in your life."

Finding purpose later in life

Finding and pursuing your purpose early on in life is to be commended. But what if those years have passed you by? Is it too late to do something purposeful and worthwhile with your life? Not necessarily.

Freda, a grandmother, found herself in this position at the age of 55. After her children had left home, through a series of chance meetings,

STEP 2: DO SOMETHING WORTHWHILE

she rediscovered her childhood faith – but with a difference. To her God was no longer a distant theory, he was a present reality. She would enthusiastically share this new-found faith with friends, relatives, neighbors and anyone else who would listen. Since then she's travelled to America a dozen times and talked to youths in the subways of Manhattan; she's spent time with tribes-people in the bush lands of Africa; she's visited Israel three times and talked with soldiers on the Golan Heights; and she's found people to chat to on her trips to Eastern Europe and Russia. As a result, many have started to think seriously about their own purpose in life and how spirituality may have a part to play in it. She's not just talked to people about God; she's talked to God about people. Experimenting with prayer, she's seen some amazing results including many who have been instantly freed from pain, others who have come off drugs going "cold turkey" with no side-effects, and one Navaho Indian woman who regained her sight.

Thinking about it, one of the benefits of spirituality is that it links you to a cause greater than yourself. Those who seek to live out their faith feel part of something bigger, something very worthwhile. They also seem to benefit from the mutual encouragement of others who share their beliefs. Additionally, when faced with challenges they tend to find an inner strength that helps them persevere in the face of difficulty.

There are many who have been called "late developers" having discovered a sense of purpose later in life. Ronald Reagan was first elected to public office at age 55; Laura Ingalls Wilder found a passion for children's stories and wrote *The Little House on the Prairie* series in her sixties; and Grandma Moses took up painting in her late seventies. It's never too late for you to find a new purpose in life.

Finding purpose in challenging times

Li had a worthwhile job helping schools and families. One day she was told her team would be restructured. Her manager was reassigned to a new project and half the team would be losing their jobs. The bombshell hit when the redundancy list was first published – which included Li's name. Initially she felt as resentful as anyone else would. She was given three months notice then her contract would be terminated. How should she handle this? Initially, begrudgingly. Over the next few days she could see her team falling apart as tensions were surfacing and the atmosphere became increasingly unpleasant. Li had a choice: she could let things deteriorate or she could take action now. She chose the latter. Leading by example, she reminded herself that her primary purpose was to serve the children and their parents within the schools she was assigned to. Next she realized no one else was going to make the effort to support her team for the next three months; they needed her more now than ever before. She had invested years into the lives of these colleagues and friends and she wasn't going to let them down now. She committed herself to being the best manager they had ever had, listening to their concerns and supporting them as they faced the biggest upheaval of their working lives to date. Even though the situation was very stressful, Li chose to look at it in a different way. She now saw this as an opportunity to help her team and develop her managerial skills, preparing her for an even better future. Whereas she previously could only see the downside of the situation, she now chose to view it as a positive learning experience. Doing so gave her a renewed sense of purpose, inner satisfaction and peace.

Redundancy and unemployment can present major challenges in life. I know, I've faced redundancy twice and joined others in the unemployment queue. People who find themselves out of work often feel a sense of loss. They can struggle to see the way forward and become disorientated in life. While they have the predictable pattern of getting up, going to work and doing what needs to be done, they can maintain some sense of purpose. Once that rhythm is broken and they are prevented from carrying on as usual, they can start to question what life is all about and what their worth is as a person. Having supported many

STEP 2: DO SOMETHING WORTHWHILE

who have found themselves the victims of redundancy and unemployment I've witnessed firsthand the truth of Kasey Edwards words in her book *30-Something and Over It*: "Working may not be the express route to happiness, but not working seems to be the fast track to unhappiness."

The solution to this problem is to find the opportunity in the difficulty. Instead of lamenting the loss of the previous job, believe that there is still something worthwhile and meaningful for you to do in life. True, it's natural to go through a grieving process as you mourn what you've lost, but don't get stuck there. Choose to move on. If you want to find new opportunities, you have to believe they are out there and look for them. You won't see them if you keep looking back over your shoulder. Think of all the good things this period of forced change has brought your way. You may have the opportunity to spend more time with friends and family, to learn a new skill, take up a new hobby, or even move area. You may choose to become more self-sufficient, take up gardening so you can grow your own food, or take a more radical step to downshift your lifestyle. Ideally, you should be thinking about both the immediate future, especially if financial survival is an issue, and the long-term. You've been given the gift of time to think. What is it you'd like to do with the rest of your life? Where do you want to go from here? As Li found, choosing a different perspective turns the whole situation around. Instead of viewing yourself as a victim of circumstances, choose to be a victor over your circumstances.

For some, making a full-time job out of looking for a full-time job gives them a sense of short-term purpose. For others, filling the time by occupying themselves in some form of voluntary or charity work seems to fill the void. It can also provide the opportunity to develop new skills and improve their feeling of self-worth as they give their time to doing something worthwhile. If you find yourself without paid employment, why not try giving some of your time to doing charitable work? It can send a signal to any future employer that you're serious about doing something worthwhile with your time. Many times people have found that temporary unpaid work has proved to be a stepping-stone to permanent paid employment.

∘∘

EXERCISE: Seeing the opportunity in unemployment
Imagine for a moment you are facing unemployment. You will now have more time on your hands than you've had for years. What might you do with yourself? Would you make a job out of finding a job? Would you give time to charitable work? Could you see yourself going back to school and learning a new skill? Capture your thoughts while they are still fresh in your mind. You might not need to follow through on them at this stage but they can still give you clues as to what you believe is a worthwhile use of your life.

∘∘

Believe in what you do, even when others don't

There may be times when you feel all alone in your pursuit of the purposeful in life. Don't worry, you're not really on your own. Many others have experienced this sense of isolation too. The main question to ask is, do you really believe that what you're doing is worthwhile?

It's encouraging when others appreciate what you're doing, but don't panic when they don't. Looking back through history there have been many that weren't fully appreciated while they were alive but became greatly respected after their death. Galileo made himself a telescope and spent many hours peering through it. He came up with lots of ideas about our solar system that people rejected because it didn't fit with what they believed at the time. Today he is hailed as one of the forefathers of modern physics. Johann Sebastian Bach was employed as a church organist playing music written by others. He wrote his own compositions in his spare time. It was 80 years after his death that Mendelssohn found some of Bach's work and through playing it helped to make Bach famous. Then there's Vincent Van Gogh who took up painting and drawing in his twenties and was virtually unknown in his own country. He produced around 2,000 works of art and though he made little money from them for most of his life, just one piece alone has recently been priced at 215 million dollars.

What value was there in peering down a tube with a disc of glass at each end? Could you justify spending hours playing on a church organ and scribbling down dots onto parchment to record the songs you dream up? Might there be a better use of your time than to sit out in the sun and paint flowers? There are countless people who invest their time and energies into their passion and will never gain recognition in their lifetimes. Don't worry if others don't fully appreciate what you're trying to do at the moment. Others might only understand and value your efforts after you've left this planet. If you believe in it, keep at it.

Go with the flow, or swim against the tide?

It takes all sorts to make a world. Like me, you've probably come across people who accept their lot in life quite willingly. Instead of focusing on the future they live more in the present. Rather than proactively planning to achieve specific goals they are more reactive and embrace life as it happens to them. They find purpose and meaning through living every day with a conscious awareness of who they are and what they need to do. There are times when I find such an accepting attitude and lack of striving quite appealing. I have great respect for anyone who can embrace their current situation and walk in peace, believing this to be their purpose in life.

Likewise, I also have respect for those who feel an inner frustration as they work so hard to change the world around them. People like Wellesley Bailey who saw the devastating effects leprosy had on people and established The Leprosy Mission that has now brought help and healing to many millions of sufferers in nearly 50 countries. Then there's Peter Chasse who founded The Water Project with a vision to bring safe, clean drinking water to the people of Africa, India and other under-developed countries. In the last six years Peter and his team have helped provide safe water to more than 500 communities. When you stop to think about it, you realize that progress happens when someone becomes dissatisfied with life as it is today. Edison would not have worked so hard to create the electric light bulb if he'd been happy to keep reading by the light of a candle. Similarly, if Alexander Graham Bell remained content to communicate by sending dots and dashes as coded signals through copper wires he wouldn't have made the effort to construct a telephone. Such people, through their continued striving, have made the world a better place.

So, some would say their purpose is to accept and live life as it is while others are not content until they've changed the world in some way. Either approach could be acceptable depending on your personal beliefs, which we'll explore further in the next chapter.

Key thoughts to take away:

Different people find their purpose in different ways and at different times in their lives. You can outwork that purpose on a full-time basis or just part-time. You might be paid for what you do or you could do it voluntarily. The key question to ask yourself is whether you believe that what you're doing is truly worthwhile or not. Other key thoughts to take away from this chapter include:

- Doing something worthwhile will make you feel happier

- Finding a cause bigger than yourself leads to greater satisfaction

- Supporting someone else's cause is just as valuable as creating your own

STEP 2: DO SOMETHING WORTHWHILE

- Giving money is purposeful
- Purpose can be discovered in everyday life
- You're never too old to find a fresh sense of purpose
- Purpose can be found in challenging times
- You can choose how to outwork your purpose

Having thought a bit about what's worthwhile in life in general, it's now time to look more specifically at what you feel is worthwhile for your own individual life. You will see things more clearly after you've worked through the next step where we look at your inner guidance system.

○ ○ ○

STEP 3:
TUNE INTO YOUR SOUL

LISTEN TO YOUR INNER GUIDANCE SYSTEM

○ ○ ○

STEP 3
Tune Into Your Soul
Listen to Your Inner Guidance System

o o o

"You were born with an inner guidance system that tells you when you are on or off purpose by the amount of joy you are experiencing. The things that bring you greatest joy are in alignment with your purpose."
(Jack Canfield – author and speaker)

o o o

Listen to your soul

NADEEM WORKED IN THE HUMAN RESOURCES department of a large organization. He was successful at what he did and helped many people day in and day out. He was well qualified and well respected. One day he came across a quote that caught his attention so he typed it out and put a copy of it on his desk. Initially it provided a sense of reassurance that what he was doing was worthwhile. As the weeks and months passed the message contained within the quote started to challenge him. He noticed a growing uneasiness within him. Eventually that quote led him to quit his job. It read:

> *The work that I shall do today is God's gift to me. Whether I am working for money or for love is irrelevant in God's sight. I can invest my energies and skills to build things that will last in my own life and in the lives of others; or I can fritter my talents away without thought or consideration. But the work that I do today is important because I have exchanged a day of my life for it. When tomorrow comes, today will be gone forever. I hope that I will not regret the return that I have received for it.*

Nadeem knew that what he was doing was worthwhile for others, but he reached the point where he felt he no longer wanted to exchange his life for the work he was being asked to do. Hearing of a part-time paid opportunity with a charitable organization he had been involved in during his spare time, he left the security of his past employment and chose instead to go and work for the charity. Somehow, from deep within, he recognized that serving his chosen charity was a better exchange of his life than working for his previous employer.

Use your intuition

When it comes to working out what you want to do with your life, many people start by looking to their intuition. Many life coaches suggest that finding your life purpose is an intuitive process. Some would suggest that you already have a clear mission in life mapped out and embedded deep within you. It's as if your purpose is encoded and hidden within your DNA or some other form of blueprint. All you have to do is look inside and find it. If you were working with an intuitive life coach it's likely they would ask you to do a few exercises to help you get in touch with your gut feelings or subconscious. One method I've seen is Steve Pavlina's "Write 'till you cry" method. He says you should take a blank piece of paper and write a question at the top of the page asking, "What could I do with my life?" Next, quickly write down an answer. Pause momentarily, then write another answer. Keep doing this until you get to the point where when you pause and reflect on what you've just written you are brought to tears. This is the thing that Steve says is most likely to be your life purpose.

o o o o o o o o o o o o o o o o o o o o o o o o o o o o o o o o o o o o o o

EXERCISE: Write 'till you cry
Try out this method by asking yourself the question "What could I do with my life?" Write your answers in your notebook. Keep writing until what you write brings you to tears. Could this be your purpose?

o o o o o o o o o o o o o o o o o o o o o o o o o o o o o o o o o o o o o o

FIND YOUR LIFE PURPOSE

This approach to getting in touch with your inner feelings is something that Peter Salovey and John Mayer researched into back in 1990. They said that our emotions can reveal things to us that our logic doesn't always see at first glance. According to them your emotions are trying to tell you something. As you pause and reflect on what you're feeling you can start to pick up clues as to what you need to pay attention to. For example, if you'd just written that one thing you could do is to feed starving children in Africa and that left you weeping, it could be that a big part of outworking your purpose could be found through serving those far less fortunate than yourself. Questions to reflect on at this stage could include, "Is there something in me that wants to feed the hungry, or is it children I want to help, or am I drawn most to the people of Africa?" It could be one or a combination of these factors. Mayer and Salovey would definitely be encouraging you to explore these things further.

Following their work, many others have invested time in trying to understand and learn from what our emotions are telling us. One of the most popular books on the subject is Daniel Goleman's title on *Emotional Intelligence*. Though much of what he says is written about using your emotions effectively to help you get on better at work, you can apply some of it to helping you find your purpose. A critical component of emotional intelligence according to Goleman is self-awareness. When you feel an inner sensation of peace you can interpret this as being on track whereas tension points to something being off track. As you learn to tune into these inner promptings you can discern what is the best way forward for you. This can be helpful as you set out to explore possible options for your life's purpose. You will be most successful, at peace and happy when you are following what your emotional intuition is pointing you towards.

Intuitive approaches can work well for some people but not necessarily for everybody. Some people are more intuitive than others. If you're not sure if you're intuitive or not you could take a personality profile test. Probably the best-known profiling test that evaluates your

STEP 3: TUNE INTO YOUR SOUL

level of intuition is the Myers-Briggs Type Indicator. After answering a series of questions based on your choices of how you would react to a range of situations, this test categorizes you into one of sixteen possible profiles based on four pairs of opposite characteristics. One of these pairs suggests that you are either an intuitive type of person, or a sensing person. Intuitive types are led more by their internal gut instincts whereas sensing types rely more on their five senses, external information, reason and logic.

But what if you're not intuitive?

If you don't consider yourself an intuitive type then using these approaches as a means to finding your purpose might not work very well for you. If this is the case then taking a more structured and investigative approach will probably work better. At first glance you might think that the Myers-Briggs approach will confine you to one of two boxes: intuitive or sensing. However, I wouldn't take such a rigid view. It's true that some people are extremely intuitive and others are far more sensing. However, research carried out by a range of people has led to the conclusion that we are a mix of both. Intuitive types often draw upon information they gather with their senses while sensing types can still pick up clues from their intuition. Rather than believing you have to fit within one of two boxes try to view this measurement as a sliding scale with high intuition and low sensing at one end and low intuition and high sensing at the other. Most of us will sit somewhere in the middle with some intuition and some sensing.

These two personality characteristics shouldn't be seen as mutually exclusive or working in opposition. Instead, consider them as working in partnership to guide you. If you start from an intuitive viewpoint and come up with an idea, use the sensing dimension of your personality to check it out and verify you are on the right track. If you rely more on your logic and reason to reach a conclusion, pause for a moment and try to work out how you feel about your intended plan. Your intuition should confirm what your rational thinking has come up with.

If you work through a number of exercises and come to a logical conclusion about what you think is worth investing your time into, but then feel uneasy about it, ask yourself "Why?" It's a sure sign that you've tapped into your intuitive side and it's trying to tell you something. Perhaps you've missed a vital piece of information. Maybe you've overestimated or underestimated something in your calculations. Whatever, it might be, don't ignore the feelings. Don't worry if you can't seem to uncover the answer immediately, sometimes your intuition bubbles through with a flash of inspiration at a later date – such as in the middle of the night when you're not using the conscious thinking side of your brain so much.

○○○○○○○○○○○○○○○○○○○○○○○○○○○○○○○○○○○○○○○

EXERCISE: Harmonising your intuitive and sensing capabilities
Next time you need to reach a decision about something try drawing upon both your intuitive and sensing capabilities. If you're an intuitive type, pause and check that your reason and logic confirm you are on track. If you see yourself as a sensing type, take a moment after you've come to a conclusion and reflect on how you feel about it.

○○○○○○○○○○○○○○○○○○○○○○○○○○○○○○○○○○○○○○○

Listening to your inner guidance system

As children, we used to play a game of hide and seek using a small object. One person would hide it and others would seek for it. When one of us got close to it the person who had hidden it would say, "You're getting hotter." If we moved further away they would say, "You're getting colder now." Did you realize that you have an inbuilt guidance system that tells you when you are getting hotter and colder in relation to what is most important to you? If you stray from your ideal path you will feel a sense

STEP 3: TUNE INTO YOUR SOUL

of discord; if you are perfectly on track you will experience inner peace and fulfilment.

Your inner guidance system can act like a satellite navigation system, speaking to you and helping you to stay on track. I believe there are three sets of signals your inner guidance system is constantly monitoring; these are your conscience, your values and your motivators. Each of these performs a slightly different function and impacts on your level of happiness and personal satisfaction, as explained below.

What's your conscience telling you?

Stewart grew up in a religious home. His family regularly went to church and were highly respected in their community. In his teens he became bored with what he felt was a restrictive lifestyle, wanting to have more fun. When he was old enough he left home and went to college in another town. In his search for excitement he started shoplifting, enjoying the thrill of outwitting others and not getting caught. One day the inevitable happened and he got caught. Facing charges, Stewart felt uncomfortable. It wasn't so much that he'd got caught, or that he would feel ashamed when facing his family, or that if he continued with his habit he could end up in even bigger trouble. No, what bothered Stewart was that deep inside, when he sat and thought about it, he knew that what he was doing was wrong. His conscience was speaking to him and he had a choice whether to listen or not. (He did listen, changed his ways, and now works in a role where he helps others live good and fulfilling lives.)

According to the English dictionary, your conscience is, "The sense of right and wrong that governs a person's thoughts and actions." Some say conscience is something we're born with, others say we acquire it as we grow up and learn about the world. Religious viewpoints normally favor the former whereas psychology seems to argue for the latter. Whichever view you take, all still agree that we have a conscience.

Conscience can be likened to a muscle; the more you exercise it the stronger it gets. When you think about your own actions you can feel discomfort concerning things you believe are wrong and integrity when you do what you know to be right. Beware though that you don't fall into the trap of self-condemnation which can be a distorted misuse of your conscience. Your conscience is designed to bring conviction, a positive realization that you shouldn't have done something you did. This empowers you to make new decisions and follow the leading of your conscience as you choose to do right next time. Self-condemnation ensnares you in excessive and unnecessary guilt. Beating yourself up over past mistakes is destructive and unhealthy, preventing you from learning and moving on. Though it can take some time and effort, the more sensitive you become to the voice of your conscience the more you will experience a growing sense of inner peace.

○○○○○○○○○○○○○○○○○○○○○○○○○○○○○○○○○○○○○○○

EXERCISE: Listening to your conscience
Pause for a moment and ask if there's anything your conscience is trying to tell you. If there's something you've said or done you feel convicted about, how can you put it right? Now remember the good things you've done. Your conscience should be reaffirming you, making you feel better on the inside.

○○○○○○○○○○○○○○○○○○○○○○○○○○○○○○○○○○○○○○○

Listen to your global conscience

Looking inwardly at your own life makes you aware of the personal dimension of your conscience. In a similar way, looking outwardly at the world around can also trigger a reaction from your conscience. Modern media brings the outside world into our own homes and bombards us repeatedly with vast quantities of global information that our minds were never designed to cope with. News programmes and documentaries inform us about the struggles and injustice others face

STEP 3: TUNE INTO YOUR SOUL

and can leave us feeling troubled yet powerless to do anything about it. Take for example a comment made by Oscar Arias Sanchez, former president of Costa Rica and Nobel Peace Prize winner who has been quoted on various news channels. During an interview for the Harvard International Review he was asked for his thoughts on the morality of spending so much money on weapons of warfare. In response he said:

> *Global expenditure on arms and soldiers is more than one trillion dollars per year. That's approximately US$3.3 billion per day. This staggering misallocation of resources is a brutal demonstration of the skewed priorities and values in many societies. We have produced one firearm for every ten inhabitants of this planet, and yet we have not bothered to end hunger when such a feat is well within our reach. By a conservative estimate, we turn out eight million small arms per year, and yet we have not managed to ensure that all our children receive a decent education. This is not a necessary or inevitable state of affairs. It is a deliberate choice.*

Such an uncomfortable fact troubles our conscience. We might not be directly responsible for the situation but we still know it is wrong and something should be done about it. What we are experiencing is a disturbing of our global or world conscience. Occasionally, individuals feel so troubled that they decide to do something about it.

In 1975 a small group of people felt so strongly about the overfishing of whales they risked their lives by sailing a small boat between the harpoons of the huge whalers and the defenceless whales. Thus was born the anti-whaling campaign arm of Greenpeace. Following further campaigning and a worldwide outcry, the International Whaling Commission banned commercial whaling just a few years later. While some commercial whaling was allowed to resume on a much smaller scale after numbers had again increased, Greenpeace has been able to help governments recognize that more profit can be made through promoting whale-watching than whale-killing. Increasingly convinced, governments are now supporting this new form of eco-tourism and discouraging commercial whaling. But it started with someone suffering from a troubled global conscience.

Some problems are so large it will take a huge international effort to resolve. Consider world hunger for a moment. Theoretically, the governments of the world could work together to fix this. Interestingly, it was the general public who came together under the inspiration of Bob Geldof that led to the huge programme known as Band Aid in 1984 and Live Aid in 1985 that helped feed many millions who were starving in Ethiopia.

It could be difficult to solve the problem of world hunger yourself, but you could easily get involved in supporting one of many projects that do. Also, you don't have to cross a vast ocean to help others who are undernourished or starving. In our own villages, towns and cities there are people that need your help. You could get involved in helping at a soup kitchen for the homeless, a meals on wheels programme feeding the elderly, or become a secret Santa leaving food parcels on the doorstep of people you know to be in need.

When tuning in to your global conscience avoid being overwhelmed. There's so much need in this world and you'll never be able to meet all of it by yourself. Having said that, there may still be something you can do to help make this world a better place. If you were to join with others who share a similar passion there's no telling what you could do. Perhaps you could become a member of a larger organization that fights for a cause you believe in. Organizations need people – and money – to enable them do what they need to do. Remember, someone had to help buy the first boat that the Greenpeace protesters sailed in.

ooooooooooooooooooooooooooooooooooooo

EXERCISE: Listening to your global conscience
When you listen to the news or watch a documentary, is there anything that troubles you or triggers you to feel compassion for others? Is your global conscience speaking to you? Do you feel a desire to do something about it? If so, make a note while it's fresh in your mind.

ooooooooooooooooooooooooooooooooooooo

STEP 3: TUNE INTO YOUR SOUL

Identify your core values

If your conscience tells you what is morally right and wrong, your core values help you recognize what is of greatest personal importance. While you may have a rough idea of what you value most, explaining this to others can sometimes prove difficult. We can get clues from looking at other people. There are things about people we like, and things we don't like. These point towards our personal values. This is true of people we know well such as family, friends and colleagues, and also people we haven't met but are aware of such as actors, musicians, politicians and others. What is it you admire in them and what do you dislike? And why is that? Here's a simple exercise to help you get started in working out what your core values are:

○○

EXERCISE: Identifying your core values
1. Write a list of qualities you respect in others, eg generosity
2. Write a new list of traits that frustrate or disappoint you, then find words to describe the opposite, eg "I dislike it when people let me down, so I value dependability"

○○

These are general values and qualities that you wish to live by. When you are living out such personal values you are at peace within yourself. You will find that you are most comfortable with other people who share these same values. Spending time with people who hold different values causes you to feel uncomfortable, even if you are not totally sure why. For example, I believe in speaking truthfully at all times. When a friend of mine told my wife a lie to provoke her and then said "I was only joking" the strength of my friendship with this individual weakened. If they continue doing this the friendship could wither and die. If they change their ways and share my value for speaking truthfully at all times then the friendship will grow stronger again.

FIND YOUR LIFE PURPOSE

Some values are more important to you than others. I value both friendship with others and also truthfulness. However, if forced to make a choice I must look to the value that means more to me. In the above case you can see that truthfulness wins out. I would rather have only a few friends that live and speak truthfully to me than have lots of people who claim to be friends but who I can't trust because they fail to speak the truth.

Subconsciously, you are making choices based on your values throughout your whole life. The clearer you are about your core values the easier it is for you to make decisions. Should you take this job or that? Would you be happier staying in the same neighborhood or moving elsewhere? If one your core values focuses on acquiring as much wealth as possible you may opt for the job with the higher salary. If a stronger value for you is based on helping others then you will take the job that gives you the opportunity to do good to those around you, even if the pay is lower. If you value stability, familiarity and maintaining current friendships you may prefer to stay living where you are. Despite that, if you have children, new values may emerge and you might consider moving to a new area that provides more opportunities for education, recreation and employment.

Your core values can change as you journey through life. Because of that, it is worth reviewing them from time to time. Circumstances happen and our view on life changes. As I'm writing this I'm reflecting on a phone call my wife received recently. It was one of her friend's sons. Apparently his mother was going for a day trip to the coast when another driver pulled out and hit her head on. She died instantly. It made us stop and think and reassess what was of most value to us. I remembered the immortal words uttered by Walter Payton, "Tomorrow is promised to no one."

Realising life has an expiry date helps you focus. In 2005 Steve Jobs (founder of Apple Computer and Pixar Animation Studios) gave a speech to graduates at Stamford University. He reflected on his recent diagnosis

STEP 3: TUNE INTO YOUR SOUL

and treatment of cancer. He told those around him, "Remembering that I'll be dead soon is the most important tool I've ever encountered to help me make the big choices in life." As a consequence he encouraged his listeners saying, "Don't let the noise of others' opinions drown out your own inner voice… have the courage to follow your heart and intuition."

Your heart and intuition draw upon your core values. Reflecting upon the possibility that we may not have as much life left as we want helps us to tune into that inner voice. At times like this we can ask ourselves what is truly most important to us. Our mind can then interpret our responses and point us in the right direction. In view of what's just been said, try the following exercise to help you focus in on your core values.

ooooooooooooooooooooooooooooooooooooooooo

EXERCISE: Refining your core values

Imagine for a moment that you were faced with a similar situation to Steve Jobs. You've visited your doctor and they tell you that you may only have six months to live. How would that change your life? What would you want to invest your remaining time and energies into? What stands out as most important now? Which of your previously identified core values remain? Are there any new ones that have surfaced? Can you place these in a relative order of importance?

ooooooooooooooooooooooooooooooooooooooooo

You may have listed "put my affairs in order". As a task, this may be a sensible priority. What I'm looking for though is the underlying value. Why do you feel you should do this? Is it to make life easier for the ones you love? If so, one of your core values could be "providing for my family". After you've made a list of those things you value most, try to put them in order, the most important at the top of your list and the least at the bottom.

Knowing your core values helps you to evaluate options and make decisions. It might be worth writing them out again and putting them somewhere where you will regularly see them. You could post them up on your kitchen door, your desk at work or the dashboard of your car. This will serve as a constant reminder to help guide your thinking and actions.

Richard, a single but very sociable man, worked as a senior clerk in a bank. Two of his core values included providing friendship and helping others less fortunate than himself. Because he did so well at work he was encouraged to join their management training programme. It didn't take him long to respond to the offer of promotion. He knew that the higher-paid job would leave him with less time and energy to give to his friends and the inner city soup kitchen where he helped out. He quickly said, "Thanks, but no thanks…" (Richard later gave up working for the bank and became a social worker where he could give more time to helping people, living a life more in line with his core values.)

Work out what motivates you

Whereas your conscience and core values provide you with a compass to help guide you as you move through life, your motivators are the source of the energy that gets you moving in the first place. Motivators are the things that prompt you to take action.

For a long time one of Chris's core values has been to live a fit and healthy lifestyle. He also believes it's good to help others. Working out regularly in the local gym, he became physically fit and regularly encouraged those around him. When he was offered a job as a fitness instructor at a nearby leisure centre he jumped at the chance. He could now be paid for doing what he enjoyed so much. One day I listened to Chris as he was explaining to a group what he did for work. He described a guy who came to him who weighed in at about 300 pounds and was suffering from low morale. Chris got him started on a gentle but structured exercise routine. This guy moved and Chris lost touch with him. One day when Chris was working in the leisure centre a stocky bloke ran over to him, picked him up and swung him around. "Thanks Chris!" he bellowed. Chris didn't recognize him. "It's me, Paul.

STEP 3: TUNE INTO YOUR SOUL

You got me started exercising again. And I feel so much better for it." In just over six months Paul had lost around 100 pounds. But it wasn't just the weight loss; his sense of self-esteem had returned and he was enjoying life again. What struck me most though was not that Chris could achieve results in the lives of others, it was the glint of moistness in his eye that said to us, "This is what moves me deep down inside. This is why I get out of bed in the morning."

Like Chris, we are usually happier when we do what we enjoy and feel is worthwhile. However, different people are motivated by different things. One person may get satisfaction from helping people, another from fixing technological problems. If you're struggling financially you'll probably be motivated by the need to earn enough to live on. If you're in the fortunate position of having more money than you require, you're more likely to be motivated towards the pursuit of leisure and pleasure. Some of our motivators are linked to our personality and core values; others are related to the circumstances we find ourselves in.

The American psychologist Abraham Maslow outlined a progression in relation to our motivators. In his Hierarchy of Needs he suggested that our basic instincts motivate us towards survival, driving us to find food, water and shelter. Once these needs are satisfied he said we then look for a community to belong to and in which to find our position. The highest level of motivator he called "self-actualization". It is at this level that people reach their full human potential and make their greatest contribution to society. I believe that those who are operating at a self-actualization level have found and are living out their life purpose.

At the lowest level, if you are struggling for survival it's unlikely that you'll be thinking about making a great contribution to the world around you. Your core values might be to live honourably and do good, but if you've not had food for two days you are much more likely to be driven towards finding something to eat. In this way, your motivators are partly dependant on your circumstances.

FIND YOUR LIFE PURPOSE

Assuming you have food, water, shelter and are part of a community, let's take a look at what else might motivate you. Understanding your motivators helps you to evaluate if you are in the right place doing the right thing or whether something needs to change. The following exercise will help you clarify your motivators. You can relate this to your work or anything else you are involved in. For many people work serves as a way of expressing yourself and what you believe to be your true purpose.

○ ○

EXERCISE: Finding your motivators – part 1
Read the six scenarios outlined below. Try to relate to them and work out which ones seem most similar to your life as it is at the moment. (It's okay to choose more than one.)

○ ○

SCENARIO 1: SIMON'S SALARY
Simon gets up early every day and sets off for work. He puts in a full 40 hours each week as he focuses on earning enough money to pay the bills and support his family. He's worked hard to get to this position and values the steady wage it provides. It's not always easy at work but he appreciates the job security. "A fair day's work for a fair day's pay is my motto. The job pays for all I need and want in life," says Simon.

SCENARIO 2: PAT'S PROGRESS
Pat works hard too. However, she wants more from work than just the money. She took this job because it offered a career pathway. If she sticks with it she could make it to area manager within the next five years. She enjoys the continual challenge, the opportunity to learn new things and gain higher-level qualifications. "This job stretches me. I feel like I'm going somewhere," says Pat.

SCENARIO 3: SHEILA'S SERVICE
Sheila didn't need to work but wanted to do something useful with

STEP 3: TUNE INTO YOUR SOUL

her time. Inspired by the example of a local foster-carer, she sought an opportunity to work as a volunteer. She was soon accepted as a carer providing short-term care for disabled children. "The work is very rewarding. It means so much to me to know I can help these children," says Sheila.

SCENARIO 4: PAUL'S PROJECT

Paul didn't need to work either. However, he enjoyed the buzz he got from doing something exciting. He took on a role as an interim project manager for a fixed term of nine months. He knew that as a temporary member of staff he would never be truly part of the team. Nonetheless, he still managed to get the project finished on time and within budget. "I enjoy work where I can use my expertise," says Paul.

SCENARIO 5: FIONA'S FRIENDSHIPS

Fiona has worked for the same employer for the past 12 years. She's made some great friends there. The Christmas party is one of the highlights of her year. As a team leader she spends a lot of time supporting other team members with their struggles and personal development. She's just been asked to organize a team away day, something she's wanted to do for ages. "My colleagues are my best friends," says Fiona.

SCENARIO 6: ANDY'S ART

Frustrated with the constraints of working for an employer, Andy set up as a self-employed artist. He knows his career prospects are minimal – as are his earnings. He's not bothered about becoming famous. His paintings are what he lives for. They reflect what he feels inside. "I was born to be free, born to be me," says Andy.

Which of these scenarios do you feel most closely reflects your current life? Usually one of these comes out stronger than the others. Each of the above focuses on a different motivator, as explained below:

Scenario	Motivator
1. Simon's salary	life needs – making sure your basic needs in life are met
2. Pat's progress	advancement – taking opportunities to improve your position in life
3. Sheila's service	altruism – serving others and meeting their needs, which in itself is satisfying
4. Paul's project	work itself – enjoying the challenge and fulfilment that the work itself provides
5. Fiona's friendships	relationships – gaining satisfaction from mutually beneficial relationships
6. Andy's art	self-expression – enjoying the chance to use your individual gifts and abilities

EXERCISE: Finding your motivators – part 2

Again, taking the above examples, if in future you could live one or more of their lives, which would appeal most to you? (Again, it's acceptable to choose more than one.)

When it comes to identifying your motivators there is no right or wrong answer. Other people in different life circumstances are likely to respond in a very different way to you. It's also common to have more than just one motivator in life. For example, you may have an underlying need to provide financially for yourself and your family and at the same time want to work in a place where you can use your talents and abilities to the full, while also being part of a friendly and supportive team.

When you compare your responses to the two parts of the exercise above, how do you feel about them? If you chose the same scenarios for both life now and the life you'd like it's probable that you feel good

STEP 3: TUNE INTO YOUR SOUL

about it. However, if your choice for the future is significantly different to life today you're likely to experience an inner tension. Maybe life is not like you'd want it to be and perhaps you need to seriously consider changing the direction you are heading in. If you're thinking about a change, try to make sure your intended course of action aligns with your motivators and core values. While they are still fresh in your mind, make a note in your notebook identifying which are your strongest motivators and any areas of life where your motivators are not being satisfied.

Rate your life satisfaction level

When you look back over your life's journey you can probably identify some hard times along the way. During tough times your happiness levels may have dipped. This is because circumstances can affect how you feel. However, it is possible to minimize these emotional dips. The secret is in how you choose to respond to what happens to you. Between the point at which you become aware of the circumstance and the moment where you respond is a period of time. Most people react instantly to difficult circumstances with feelings of frustration, anger, fear or sadness. However, you don't have to react this way, instead you can choose to pause and think about it. This pause enables you to look at the circumstance from different angles. You may ask questions like, "What's really happening here? How will this affect me and those around me? What are my options for handling this situation?" Taking an objective stance like this will help you cope better and you will respond more positively. Often, the longer the pause, the more effective your response will be.

Whereas your happiness is a temporary state that can be affected by your circumstances, your level of true satisfaction in life is an underlying condition that is governed mainly by your conscience, values and motivators. If your conscience is troubled, or you recognize that you are not living in accordance with your values, or your motivators are not being satisfied, you will feel dissatisfied. You may not recognize it immediately but you will still know something is wrong. For example, if you were hoping for promotion at work but the job is given to someone else, as soon as you hear the news you can immediately become unhappy. Alternatively, you could have a well-paid job you enjoy but feel increasingly uneasy. On reflection you could realize something is out of alignment. You joined the organization because you believed they were providing a much-needed service to a particular group of people – and they were. However, you are now aware that their primary concern is to make money for their shareholders. To some extent, it doesn't matter if it's the company that's changed or if they've always been like that and you've only just found out; the fact is you now feel an inner conflict. When you become aware of a misalignment between life and your conscience, values or motivators, something happens at a deeper level. If you don't address this you will grow increasingly dissatisfied. This can't be fixed by doing something that gives you a temporary high in your happiness levels, like eating chocolate or drinking alcohol. You need to do something more radical, like change your life.

Personal reflection

○○○○○○○○○○○○○○○○○○○○○○○○○○○○○○○○○○○○○○

EXERCISE: Life satisfaction levels

Thinking back over your life, when did you feel most satisfied? Why was that? Compare that to life as it is today. How satisfied do you feel right now in life? If you don't feel fully satisfied, do you intuitively sense why? Is your conscience trying to tell you something? How closely are you living in relation to your core values? How well are your motivators being satisfied? Is there anything that needs to change? Note down your answers in your notebook. This is important. You may need to come back to these things and work through them in more detail.

○○○○○○○○○○○○○○○○○○○○○○○○○○○○○○○○○○○○○○

STEP 3: TUNE INTO YOUR SOUL

> **Key thoughts to take away:**
>
> We all have an inner guidance system. Learning to tune into your soul will help you work out what is most purposeful for you as an individual. Key thoughts to take away from this chapter include:
>
> - Your intuition can lead you to discover your purpose
>
> - Check that your intuition and reason are working in harmony
>
> - You can learn to listen to your conscience
>
> - Knowing and living according to your core values will give you an inner peace
>
> - Working out what motivates you helps you to choose the right way forward
>
> - If your life satisfaction level is lower than you want it to be, do something about it!
>
> Having tuned into your conscience, identified your core values and understood your motivators, another important area is to explore is that of your hopes and dreams. That's what the following chapter will help you to do.

o o o

STEP 4:
WAKE UP TO YOUR DREAMS

EXPLORE YOUR HIDDEN HOPES

STEP 4
Wake Up To Your Dreams
Explore Your Hidden Hopes

o o o

"All men dream, but not equally. Those who dream by night in the dusty recesses of their minds, wake in the day to find that it was vanity: but the dreamers of the day are dangerous men, for they may act on their dreams with open eyes, to make them possible."
(T E Lawrence – soldier and writer)

o o o

Living the dream

BOB AND MARY HAD A DREAM: to build their own house and live a self-sufficient lifestyle in the quiet countryside where their children could run free within their own smallholding. When they saw a building plot with adjoining fields overlooking a grassy valley come on the market, they decided this was just what they were looking for. They went to auction and with a bit of help from family managed to buy it. Selling their previous cottage, they then set up home in a caravan on the side of a hill. Mary happily gave up the office job she was becoming bored with and Bob shut up shop on his small business so they could focus full-time on building their new life.

Growing their own food was a priority so they quickly cultivated a garden that could provide them with a variety of fruit, vegetables and herbs. Setting up a poly-tunnel gave them the opportunity to experiment with a wider range of foods and extend their growing season.

STEP 4: WAKE UP TO YOUR DREAMS

Another investment they made was a big freezer to help store the food they couldn't eat straight away. They also learnt to make pickles and chutney as a way to preserve food. Added to that, they experimented with keeping chickens, ducks and pigs, many of which also found their way into the freezer.

In line with their vision of living more sustainability, they've planted several thousand trees which have become a source of fuel for their wood-burning stove. Water comes from a borehole they've sunk on their land and electricity is provided by their two wind turbines. They sell the excess electricity they generate back to the Electricity Board and Bob also sells logs, the income paying for other bills and things they can't grow themselves.

Working from sunrise to sunset, it's a physically demanding lifestyle but they are more than compensated by the emotional rewards. They've learnt to work in harmony with the seasons so look forward to the longer winter evenings when they can curl up with a good book in front of their warming fire. Chatting with them in their open-plan kitchen-diner one dark evening, I did wonder if they had found a better balance in life than the rest of us who follow the pattern of modern living that expects us to work at full speed for all twelve months of the year.

It took three years before Bob and Mary could move out of their caravan and into their hand-built home. Perhaps one of the features that Bob is most proud of is the bread oven he made that's hidden in a sheltered part of the garden. On a mild autumn evening Bob, Mary and their children can enjoy sitting out and warming themselves by the oven as it slowly bakes them a homemade pizza for their tea.

Choosing such a lifestyle has its consequences. For transport Bob has an old pick-up that he uses to tow trailers full of logs he sells. The family don't enjoy many of the luxuries we may take for granted such as the latest design in clothes or holidays overseas. As they've sought to minimize their own expenditure they've also learnt new skills including being able to cut their own hair! They admit they have sometimes felt overwhelmed by how much work there is to do. Then there are times they've been a little frustrated with themselves that they aren't totally self-sufficient. They confessed to having bought potatoes this year when their own garden failed to produce them. However, the simple pleasures of life they enjoy such as eating fresh food straight from their garden, drinking their own homemade cider and walking their dog beside the stream at the bottom of their own field far outweighs any drawbacks.

It's been 14 years since Bob and Mary took the decision to change direction and set out to create the life of their dreams. In doing so they aimed to live a simpler and more sustainable life and focus more on enjoying quality time together as a family. With all the hard work that's been demanded of them, has it been worth it? In their own words, "Oh yes, totally. You get a great feel good factor. There's always something new to learn and new projects to do. And we're sure the children will be able to look back on this time and appreciate it." And their advice to others who want to live a dream life like theirs? "Be prepared to give up some things and cut back on luxuries. Be patient but remain focused and positive. It might be hard work but there's never a dull moment. It's definitely worth it."

Passions and dreams

Whereas dreams focus more on the future, passions relate mainly to the present. Some people are passionate about sport, others music or art, yet others a hobby or pastime. Such passions reveal insights as to what we both value and find interesting. Some people have been able to make a living from pursuing their passion. Cindy had a passion for scrapbooking. Her hobby grew and so did her expertise. After just a few years it seemed quite natural for her to take the step of opening a small craft shop. She then passed on her enthusiasm and skills to others who wanted to learn from her through the training workshops she set up. Her passion became a profitable business.

STEP 4: WAKE UP TO YOUR DREAMS

A passion can develop into a dream. As a child, Elisabeth loved donkeys. However, it was only in 1969 after she left home and got married that she was able to own one of her own. Her passion grew and she became an Area Representative for the Donkey Breed Society. Seeing a neglected donkey at a market in Devon she felt moved to change her focus from breeding donkeys to rescuing them. By 1973 her little sanctuary was caring for 38 donkeys. The following year she received a gift from the estate of a similar sanctuary – an additional 204 donkeys. Elisabeth then formed a new charity, The Donkey Sanctuary, and since that time her team has cared for nearly 15,000 donkeys in the UK and Ireland alone. Elisabeth had a passion, it grew into a dream, and that dream transformed the lives of thousands of animals.

Your passions can become dreams and your dreams can become a full-time business. You don't have to start a business though. Many have found their dream job where they've been able to do what they loved doing and get paid for it. Julie loved animals and found work as a vet's assistant, Farah enjoyed being around children and helping them learn and gained employment as a primary school teacher, and Chris who we've already mentioned landed a job as a fitness instructor. It's good to be passionate about what you do in life. If you're not sure what your passions are and would like a bit of help to identify them, try out the following exercise.

○○○○○○○○○○○○○○○○○○○○○○○○○○○○○○○○○○○○

EXERCISE: Exploring your passions
Take a few minutes to explore your passions. Try answering the following questions. Again, capture any useful thoughts that come out of your reflection.

1. *What would you do even if you weren't paid for doing it?*
2. *When in conversation with others, what subjects get you most excited?*
3. *When you've been so engrossed in something that time just disappears, what is it you were doing?*

4. *If you could do anything and you were guaranteed to succeed at it, what would you want to do?*

5. *If you could swop jobs with anyone else, who would it be and why? (Make sure you focus on what they do and not just the benefits they get from what they do, such as the salary.)*

○ ○

What is your dream?

Back in 1982 Captain Sensible wrote a best-selling song called *Happy Talk*. One line he repeated several times was, "If you don't have a dream, how you gonna make a dream come true?" Though some dismissed the song as being shallow and almost nonsensical, this one line drives home a serious point. We need dreams. We can't make dreams come true unless we dream them in the first place.

Stephen Covey's second habit from his book *The Seven Habits of Highly Effective People* states you should, "Start with the end in mind." Having a dream gives you something to work towards. It provides you with an end to aim for. Once you know where you are going you can work out how to get there. Similarly, in the GROW model of coaching the first step is to identify your Goal. It's only after that you look at your current Reality. If you start with where you are today you are more likely to limit yourself because of your current reality. If you start with your dream you will then have something to aspire to and head for.

Some people are very clear about what their dream is. If you ask them to describe their ideal life in future their eyes light up and they paint you a wonderful word picture. Others find it a bit more difficult to articulate. If you're struggling to identify a dream at this stage of your life it can sometimes pay to wind back the clock and think about your childhood dreams. When you were younger and adults asked you what you wanted to be when you grew up, how did you answer them? Did

STEP 4: WAKE UP TO YOUR DREAMS

you say you wanted to be a firefighter, or a nurse, maybe an explorer or a famous sports person? These childhood dreams can give us clues. They reveal something about what we considered to be important at the time. Perhaps they showed we wanted to be part of a team doing something to help others. Possibly they pointed to us having a desire to achieve or succeed in facing and overcoming challenges. Could it have been that you knew someone who was fulfilling a certain role and you really respected them for who they were and what they were doing?

○○○○○○○○○○○○○○○○○○○○○○○○○○○○○○○○○○○○○○○

EXERCISE: Reviewing your childhood dreams

1. *What dreams did you have when you were younger? (Becoming a firefighter.)*
2. *What was it that appealed to you about them? (Heroically rescuing people.)*
3. *What does this say about you as a person? (You like action and excitement, to be part of a dynamic team and to do something important to help others.)*
4. *What can you learn from the above to help you clarify your future dreams? (I want to do something that I feel is more purposeful to help others, being part of a dynamic team where we can see results for our actions.)*

○○○○○○○○○○○○○○○○○○○○○○○○○○○○○○○○○○○○○○○

As well as looking backwards in time, you can also get some insights from the present that can help you to shed light on your dream. One place to look at is your interests and hobbies. If you're watching television, what programmes interest you? What magazines do you buy? If you go to a library or browse online bookstores what books are you attracted to? Supposing you went to a party and someone asked you what you were interested in, what would you tell them? All of these can give clues as to where your dreams lie. Make a note in your notebook of any areas where you have a strong interest or passion.

When we talk about dreams, we shouldn't overlook what goes through our minds as we sleep. According to Ian Wallace, an expert with more than thirty years of dream interpretation experience:

The dreams you create are stories that express everything you are unconsciously aware of and reflect what you find most meaningful in waking life. These stories are the natural language of your unconscious awareness and have a deeper wisdom and a broader understanding than your conscious self.

Being able to capture and interpret what our unconscious (or subconscious) mind is telling us can again help us to identify our hidden dreams. Native American Indians used to make something they called dream catchers. A wooden hoop covered with a woven loose net or web, they believed this device helped sleeping people capture and retain their good dreams. Whether or not it worked in one sense is immaterial; the Indians recognized the value of capturing good dreams and hanging on to them. A modern equivalent is to keep a notepad and pen beside your bed. When you wake up, if you've been dreaming, try recording any dreams you remember before you move into the busyness of the day and lose them. Moving with the times, did you know you can now get an app for your Apple iPhone to help you capture and record your dreams?

ooooooooooooooooooooooooooooooooooooooooooo

EXERCISE: Dream-catching
If you find you can recall your dreams try writing them down. Look for patterns or repeated themes. Are there any that stand out to you as more vivid than others? If this is an area you would like to learn more about there are several helpful books that explain the possible symbolic meaning of your dreams.

ooooooooooooooooooooooooooooooooooooooooooo

When dreams are put on hold

Sometimes the dreams we grew up with were cut off in their prime. When Jo was in her teens she enjoyed art. Marrying young, she quickly became pregnant and found her life changing radically. The following years revolved around caring for her family and working part-time to

STEP 4: WAKE UP TO YOUR DREAMS

help provide some income. Many years later, she found herself single again, her husband having left her and her daughter moving away for a career opportunity. Jo returned to college to pursue her passion for art again. Gaining a formal qualification, she displayed her work at a number of galleries and exhibitions. Interestingly, she found her work sold better when she displayed it in galleries close to where her daughter lived. Having found a responsive market for her unique blend of art she then chose to relocate to live nearer her daughter. Jo's dream of becoming an artist was originally put on hold for her family but has now become a means by which she can support herself and live closer to her daughter – and new baby granddaughter.

Tim had a passion for fast cars. He enjoyed them so much he managed to find himself a job as a mechanic in a sports car dealership. He dreamed of owning his own garage where could tune them to go even faster. Then he injured himself at work. Tim had to face the facts; it was very unlikely he could continue as a sports car mechanic. He retrained, took a business studies course and found a well-paid office job. Even though he became successful in his second career he knew deep down that this wasn't what he wanted to do with his life. Now middle-aged, he knows he won't be able to go back to being a youthful, energetic mechanic. However, Tim's been thinking lately, he could apply his office-based commercial experience and set up his own business where he manages mechanics that do the hard work for him. He can be the brains behind the brawn. His dream, once cut off, could live again.

Sometimes life's circumstances lead us down pathways we wouldn't have chosen for ourselves. Instead of taking to the open road we find ourselves directed down a diversion. Dreams we once cherished become closeted, hidden away and forgotten. Life has its twists and turns, many of which we couldn't have foreseen. For some though, as the years pass, opportunity arises for us to get back on track and pick up where we left off from our original journey. Jo did this with her art. For others though, they can never go back to where they once were. Instead, by reinterpreting the landscape of life, they may see a new way forward. Tim's thinking of doing this with his passion for sports cars. As he contemplates starting his own business he could end up living a modified dream, not as a mechanic, but as a manager of mechanics.

You need wisdom when reviewing your past dreams; some can be continued, others adapted, and some may be better placed to one side for the moment – or even laid to rest. We mature as we age (hopefully) and life changes us. What may have been appropriate when we were twenty might no longer be so once we reach forty or fifty. Jo put her dream of being an artist to one side for a while but was able to pick it up again. By contrast, Brian, a promising young swimmer, had to give up his hopes of competing professionally after sustaining a serious leg injury.

There may be occasions when it appears wiser to follow your dream as a part-time hobby rather than pursuing it as a career. Nick loved pottery so went back to college to study ceramics and gain a higher-level qualification. He also bought himself a small kiln with which to fire his pots. Talented as he was, he soon discovered many others also enjoyed pottery – making it that is, not necessarily buying it. He sold a few of his creations, but not as many as he had hoped for. He also found some part-time teaching work through the local college where he passed on his skill to others. However, there was no way he could make a living from it. His disappointment at not being able to support himself financially took some of the fun out of his work. It was time for a rethink. He decided to remove the burden of trying to use it as a way to make a living. Instead, by approaching it as a hobby again Nick has been able to see pottery as a satisfying hobby once again.

ooooooooooooooooooooooooooooooooooooooo

EXERCISE: Dreams on hold

Do you have any dreams that you have put on hold? Are you able to pick them up and run with them again? Or can you pursue them as a part-time hobby? Or do you need to face the hard facts, lay them aside and move on? Jot down anything relevant you conclude in your notebook.

○ ○

Don't suppress your dreams

Some people stop themselves before they can start. They have a dream hidden deep within them but they refuse to let it come to the surface. Why is that? Sometimes it's because they're apprehensive when it comes to talking to others about it. If you come from humble origins then you may be afraid others will laugh at you if you share with them your dream of doing something significant with your life. It could be that your friends lack the imagination or belief that they could do what you're dreaming of doing. Or some may feel envy that you might do something significant with your life while they're just drifting along. Others may be afraid they will lose your friendship so they actively discourage you from breaking away to do something new. Because of this peer pressure, you could choose to suppress your dream in an effort to maintain the current friendship. If your fear of losing the friendship is greater than the value you place on your dream, you're likely to put it down before you pick it up.

Then there's the possibility that you may be sabotaging yourself when you think of the sheer scale of what you could achieve once you set your mind to it. The problem isn't to do with what other people may think about you, it's to do with what you think about you. You may even doubt your right to be so bold as to dream a big dream. Peace activist and author of *Return to Love*, Marianne Williamson, put it like this:

> *Our deepest fear is not that we are inadequate. Our deepest fear is that we are powerful beyond measure. It is our light, not our darkness that most frightens us. We ask ourselves, Who am I to be brilliant, gorgeous, talented, fabulous? Actually, who are you not to be? You are a child of God. Your playing small does not serve the world. There's nothing enlightened about shrink-*

ing so that other people won't feel insecure around you. We are all meant to shine, as children do. We were born to make manifest the glory of God that is within us. It's not just in some of us; it's in everyone. And as we let our own light shine, we unconsciously give others permission to do the same. As we are liberated from our own fear, our presence automatically liberates others.

Try looking at it this way. By giving yourself permission to pursue your dream you can inspire others to attempt something worthwhile with their lives also. I'm sure you'll feel happier if you set out to do something you're passionate about and believe in. You will benefit, your friends will benefit, and the world around you will benefit when what you're attempting to do is worthwhile. So if you've been suppressing a dream, I'd say now is the time to face up to it and work out why you've been doing so. What are you gaining by holding back? What more could you gain from moving forward? If you've been waiting for someone to give you permission to once again explore your suppressed dream, today is the day, now is the moment. Right now I give you permission to explore your suppressed dreams!

○○○○○○○○○○○○○○○○○○○○○○○○○○○○○○○○○○○○○○○

EXERCISE: Exploring suppressed dreams
Have you found it difficult to talk to others about your dreams? Why is that? Or are you overwhelmed by the huge possibility of your own potential? Try drawing up two lists, the first identifying what you've got to gain by continuing to suppress your dream; the other noting what the possibilities could be if you were to pursue your dream. If fear is holding you back in some way, we'll be looking at how to overcome it in a later chapter.

○○○○○○○○○○○○○○○○○○○○○○○○○○○○○○○○○○○○○○○

Review your dreams

When your dreams don't live up to their original expectations, review them! For some people living the dream doesn't always work out as

STEP 4: WAKE UP TO YOUR DREAMS

first planned. Nigel's faith was so important to him he decided to make it his vocation. Giving up his job he went to college for two years to pursue his dream of becoming a church minister. Following graduation he moved to a different part of the country with his wife and children to take up the role of Assistant Church Minister. It was a mixed experience, very rewarding but also very challenging. After three hard years he paused to reflect on and review his dream. He identified what he liked most about the job – which was helping young children learn. Nigel then chose to relocate closer to family and retrain once more, but this time as a primary school teacher. Working for a local school, he has now found a role in life that suits him much better. Coincidentally, the church they chose to attend has now asked if Nigel and his wife can help out on the leadership team. They seem to have found a balance that meets the needs of the whole family and has enabled Nigel to discover and pursue a new dream. He doesn't regret those previous five years spent in training and church ministry, quite the opposite, they helped him clarify and prepare for an even better future.

Like Nigel, it might take you some time and a couple of attempts before you find what you are truly searching for. Don't be too disappointed if you discover your initial dream doesn't live up to your expectations. There have been many musicians who have loved their music but in seeking to turn professional discovered pressures and politics within the music industry that led to disillusionment rather than greater enjoyment. Definitely, I'd encourage you to pursue your passion, but be aware there may be unexpected challenges along the way. If your dreams don't seem to be working out as planned, pause, ask yourself why and what you can learn from your experiences. Like Nigel, you may need to take stock of the situation, review your dream and find a new way forward. Remember, no previous experience is wasted if you can learn from it.

Mark and Sarah's dream was to live a quiet life in the South of England. When his company downsized Mark was told he was "redundant".

As well as throwing himself headlong into searching for a new job, Mark decided now was the opportune time to give his wife the holiday of a lifetime. They flew to New Zealand and spent a happy month in the sun. While there they met a number of English families who had emigrated and it started them thinking. Returning to the UK with no job prospects on the horizon, they reviewed their dream. Mark found a suitable job in New Zealand and within months they had sold their house and were back in Auckland.

Like many in life, Mark isn't set on changing the world. He believes his main purpose in life is to live a decent life and provide for his family. However, following an unexpected twist of fate both he and Sarah gave themselves permission to find a new expression of how to do just that, but this time on the other side of the world. Their only regret is that they hadn't reviewed their dream earlier.

It's not uncommon to review your dreams and direction in midlife. In their book, *Midlife, a Manual*, Steven and Judith Estrine talk about those who consciously decide to change their dreams as they go through life. They point out:

> *There are lots of reasons why people change their life's direction in midlife: financial, personal, circumstantial. Some of the people to whom we spoke seemed to be made of whole cloth. They were born knowing what they wanted from life and went on to pursue the dream. For many however, life has been a series of compromises, disappointments and re-evaluations. Midlife is a time when we once again re-evaluate the course we have taken. The world has changed since we were young, and so have we. Midlife is a time to reassess where we are and what we want for the next thirty-five years.*

So it's okay if you want to park one dream and drive off in another. Don't feel that because you started out with one dream in life you are bound to it forever. Having a midlife crisis is quite normal. If you're in the middle of one see it as an opportunity, the chance to re-evaluate life and find a new way forward. Sure, there's always a risk when you step out onto a path you've not trodden before, but maybe there's a bigger risk if you try to stick to the path you've been walking on for years.

Find a new dream

Sometimes you can outgrow your dream. Did your dreams change as you grew up? As you aged your dreams may have also matured. Instead of still wanting to be a fire-fighter rescuing one or two people, perhaps you now visualize yourself as an environmental activist locked into a battle against global warming that threatens the population of the entire world. If your dreams have changed, is there still an underlying theme to them? What does that tell you?

There's something else about dreams many have discovered. When your dream lies within sight but just beyond your reach, you work hard to take hold of it. There's something exciting about living with hope as you strive to achieve your goal. Your inner desire draws you on and helps you maintain momentum. However, once you've achieved the dream it's possible for your feelings to change. Having gained what you so eagerly sought your original motivation can leave you. The challenge has gone and so often the passion that accompanied it. When you lose the desire for the thing you've been striving for you can become restless and start looking for something new. Some people are able to dedicate themselves to a single cause for the whole of their lives; others look for a variety of causes or challenges to pursue. It's possible that you too could outgrow your dreams. Working with a number of motivated achievers Judith Leary-Joyce recognized a trend and had this to say:

> *Passion – or the lack of it – also explains why restlessness can suddenly set in. There is nothing like working in an arena that excites and inspires you. It builds energy all on its own and you achieve beyond your wildest dreams. Having such a wonderful time also makes it hard to carry on when the flame has gone out. Once the desired outcome is achieved, it*

is time to move on to something that gets the spark going again. This is the story of serial achievement: do work that matters — for as long as it matters — then move on.

If you've achieved the goals you've previously set yourself and the passion has evaporated, perhaps it's time for you to set new goals or dream a new dream. Consider moving on from where you are now.

Chasing more than one dream

From time to time I meet people who have a range of interests and things they want to do in life. For them, being tied to just one dream would be frustrating. The solution is to pursue multiple dreams. If that's you there are two pathways you might want to consider:

1. PARALLEL DREAM CHASING:
With parallel dream chasing you go after several things at the same time. This keeps life interesting and varied. Something you'll find with this approach is that it's harder to make a lot of progress in one area at a time as your attention and effort is spread across a range of activities. Depending on your personality, you may want to approach this in a structured way, allocating set amounts of time to each dream. One method is to give time to each dream a bit like a traditional school day broken up into set lessons. Or you could work at them like a farmer who watches the seasons and focuses on different aspects of their work at different times of the year. Alternatively, you may be more fluid in your approach, drifting from one dream to the other as the mood takes you.

Some life coaches would encourage this approach. They would ask you to set goals for several areas of life at the same time. One would be to reach a new level of fitness and health, another would be linked to career development, personal relationships with friends and relatives would also be targeted, as may psychological and spiritual wellbeing.

STEP 4: WAKE UP TO YOUR DREAMS

2. SEQUENTIAL DREAM CHASING

Sequential dream chasing takes a bit more discipline. Having identified the various things you want to do in life you need to get them in some kind of order. Once you've worked out what you want to do first you commit yourself to it and stick at it until you've achieved it. Then you move on to the next dream. This takes more discipline. When there are other appealing projects on your longer-term to-do list it's easy to become distracted – especially if your current project is presenting you with a challenge. The temptation is to give up and move on to the next thing.

There may be times when actually parking the current project and coming back to it later may make sense. Some writers find this happens when they reach an impasse. Taking a break to do something different for a while frees up their mind and allows them to return to their writing with fresh inspiration.

○○

EXERCISE: Multiple dreams
Do you have more than one dream? If so, which approach might suit you better? Would you want to pursue more than one dream at a time? Or would you prefer to tackle them one at a time? If this is relevant to you, try to determine which approach might work best for you and make a new note in your notebook.

○○

Dream a bigger dream

Sometimes I think we dream too small. We limit ourselves and what we believe we are capable of by our own thinking. By limiting ourselves we fail to reach our full potential and the world is a poorer place. If you've not dreamed before I'd encourage you to start dreaming. If you've only let yourself dream small dreams then I'd challenge you to expand the size of your dreams. Dreaming big dreams can be good not just for you but also those around you. When Martin Luther King Jr stood on the steps of the Lincoln Memorial in Washington DC and said "I have a dream..." the impact was felt across the whole of America. He challenged the racial segregation and discrimination that was present at the time and as a result became the youngest person ever to receive the Nobel Peace Prize. King used to read poetry written by Henry David Thoreau. Perhaps it may have been Thoreau's words that inspired King when he said, "If one advances confidently in the direction of his dreams, and endeavors to live the life which he has imagined, he will meet with success unexpected in common hours."

Don't worry if others think your dream is illogical or impossible. People who dream big dreams aren't put off by the opinion of others. People used to believe it was risky to sail out too far into the ocean just in case they fell off the edge of the world. Then in 1522 Juan Sebastián Elcano, Ferdinand Magellan's second in command, returned from a voyage that took him all the way around the earth. Less than 200 years ago you would have been laughed at if you said you could foresee hundreds of people flying through the air together both faster and higher than the birds. But the Wright brothers led the way with powered flight. Then there's the science fiction stories of the early 1900s that told of men going into space that became science fact within just a few short decades.

Dreams are created as a theory in the mind before they become a reality on the ground. They start off as a psychological possibility and only later turn into a physical actuality. W Clement Stone, author of *Believe and Achieve*, was well aware of this when he said, "Whatever the mind of man [or woman] can conceive and believe, it can achieve." To see something manifest in the world around you, you first need to visualize it in your mind within you. The external world is shaped by your internal world. Dreamers of big dreams aren't limited by their current level of knowledge or the opinions of others. Instead, they focus on what they want to do and lean heavily on the age-old saying, "Where there's a will there's a way."

STEP 4: WAKE UP TO YOUR DREAMS

Are you starting to recognize that you are capable of not only more than you're currently doing, but more than you think you could do? If you aim for the stars but only reach the moon, you've still travelled further than most people on this earth. How big is your dream? Is it time for you to think about dreaming a bigger dream?

Write your bucket list

In the 2007 film *Bucket List*, working-class mechanic Carter Chambers (Morgan Freeman) and billionaire businessman Edward Cole (Jack Nicholson) are brought together by tragic circumstances, having both just been diagnosed with cancer. At first, there is tension between them as they struggle to relate to each other. Having been told he has less than a year to live, Carter recalls the advice of his college tutor who many years previously had encouraged his class to write down what they wanted to do and where they wanted to go before they "kicked the bucket". Carter wrote his list, then screwed it up and threw it away. Edward discovers it and persuades Carter to go for it, adding a few ideas of his own. As their friendship quickly grows they agree to use the time they have left to pursue their dreams together. Funded by Edward they go car racing, climb the pyramids, skydive and ride a motorcycle along the Great Wall of China.

It wasn't just about having a good time though, through their friendship Carter got Edward to think more seriously about life. This led to Edward being reconciled to his estranged daughter and newborn granddaughter. The former harsh businessman mellowed and in chasing his dreams he discovered more depth of meaning and purpose in his life. It was through creating this list they gave themselves permission to explore their dreams, leading to greater fulfilment in life.

○○○○○○○○○○○○○○○○○○○○○○○○○○○○○○○○○○○○○○

EXERCISE: Write your bucket list
Give yourself at least 40 minutes to work through this exercise. Facing the fact that your time on earth is limited, find yourself a pen and paper and write

out your bucket list. Aim to complete the following sentence with at least fifty but ideally one hundred things you would like to do or see in the remainder of your lifetime.

"In the time that I have left I would like to..."

The reason for aiming for a list of one hundred is to help draw out any hidden hopes and dreams you don't normally think about. Again, it's relatively easy to find ten or twenty things you would like to do and a dozen places you would like to see. It's much harder to find one hundred. Once you've written your list look over it and see what you notice. Are there any repeated patterns? What new ideas have come to mind? Have you spotted any childhood dreams? Again, use your notebook to capture your observations.

○ ○

Key thoughts to take away:

We all have dreams, even if they are hidden or suppressed. Acknowledging and contemplating our dreams can direct us towards a greater understanding of what our life purpose may be. Key thoughts to take away from this chapter include:

- You can live the dream
- You need a dream to make a dream come true
- Don't be afraid to dream big dreams
- You can chase more than one dream
- You have permission to change your dream
- It's never too soon to write your bucket list
- Ask yourself, "How can I make my dream a reality?"

STEP 4: WAKE UP TO YOUR DREAMS

> Being more aware of your dreams can give you clarity about which direction to head off in. Later we'll explore how you can plan to turn your dream into reality. Before you set off though, it will pay to think a bit about your current capabilities. The next chapter will help you to look at these, but maybe from a different angle.

○ ○ ○

STEP 5:
PLAY TO YOUR STRENGTHS

MAKE THE MOST OF YOUR SKILLS AND ABILITIES

○ ○ ○

STEP 5

Play To Your Strengths
Make The Most of Your Skills and Abilities

o o o

"Success is achieved by developing our strengths, not by eliminating our weaknesses."
(Marilyn vos Savant – writer and lecturer)

o o o

What are your strengths?

MOST PEOPLE WRITING ON THE SUBJECT of personal development and success would agree with the above; do what you are good at and it's easier to succeed. Some time ago the University of Nebraska undertook a study to find the most effective way to teach speed reading. Within a period of three years 1,000 students took a course in speed reading utilising a range of tutors and techniques. As they expected, the better teachers saw the greatest improvement in their students. What surprised them though was the difference between the rate of improvement in different types of learners. Whereas those starting with a low speed of 90 words per minute increased by nearly four times to 350 words, the speed of the faster students who started with a level of 350 words per minute shot up by more than eight times to 2,900 words. One of their most powerful conclusions from the study was that people should be encouraged to work with and play to their strengths.

If you already recognize your strengths then this step may appear fairly straightforward at first sight. However, even if you already know what you are good at, you can still benefit from this chapter. It might be

STEP 5: PLAY TO YOUR STRENGTHS

that you're not enjoying working with your strengths as much as you used to or you could be unaware of other hidden talents you possess. Working through this step will shed light on your skills and abilities in a new way and help you appreciate your strengths more fully.

Why education doesn't guarantee success

Modern society places much emphasis on the importance of education. Those achieving higher grades are usually expected to make more of their lives than those who don't. When I went to school there was something called the 11-plus examination. Those that passed went to the local grammar school; the other children went to the secondary modern. At the end of secondary school the better paying employers such as banks, solicitors and accountants favored recruiting from the grammar schools. Young people from the secondary modern usually thought more about going to work in one of the local factories or becoming an apprentice in a practical trade.

Many years later, it is interesting to see what has happened to those young people. You would expect the ex-grammar school children to have secured the better paying jobs with the more promising futures. In some cases that has been so – but not always. Some of the secondary modern kids ended up learning a trade then left their employers to set up their own businesses. Through hard work and willingness to take a risk, they have prospered more than many of the children who were previously thought of as having greater intelligence.

With the recent recession, a number who went to work with the professional service employers or for the public sector have found their jobs to be extremely vulnerable. Phil, a senior manager who worked for a council, was recently made redundant. After several months of searching for a new job he was offered a post as a part-time clerk at a neighboring council. The wage is equivalent to what he earned when he first left school. Phil found that having a good education and a reasonable level of intelligence does not guarantee a successful long-term career or short-term job security.

You're intelligent in more ways than one

Our modern education system has been built around measuring one form of intelligence known as your "Intelligence Quotient", or IQ. If you're good at passing exams this works in your favor. There are others though who are better at practical tasks or competing in sports. Harvard University professor Howard Gardner described his concept of "multiple intelligences" in his book *Frames of Mind*. He felt that there was too much focus on a narrow spectrum of skills development in traditional education. Schools didn't always cater for young people who seemed to be gifted in other ways. From his initial research he identified seven forms of intelligence which he called:

1. **Linguistic intelligence** – being able to learn or use language well. Examples include writers, speakers, lawyers and talk show hosts.

2. **Logical-mathematical intelligence** – being able to solve problems and work with numbers. Examples include accountants, scientists and computer programmers.

3. **Musical intelligence** – being able to recognize, compose and present musical patterns. Examples include singers, musicians and songwriters. (This is often linked closely to linguistic intelligence.)

4. **Bodily-kinaesthetic intelligence** – being able to use your mind to skilfully control your body movements. Examples include dancers, actors and athletes.

5. **Spatial intelligence** – being able to appreciate and work with spaces. Examples include architects, graphic designers and town planners.

STEP 5: PLAY TO YOUR STRENGTHS

6. **Interpersonal intelligence** – being able to understand and work effectively with other people. Examples include teachers, counsellors and leaders of organizations.

7. **Intrapersonal intelligence** – being able to understand yourself and your own motivations, fears, etc. This helps you to manage yourself more effectively.

Gardner later added to this list with an eighth form of intelligence that he called naturalistic intelligence. This describes the ability you may have to sense patterns and relate to elements within the natural world around you. People displaying such intelligence could include farmers, vets, environmental scientists and gardeners.

Did the world you grow up in give more attention to just one or two of these intelligences such as mathematics and language skills, while largely ignoring the others? What if your strongest form of intelligence has not been catered for at school or work? Could it be that you have felt frustrated, like a square peg in a round hole, when what you needed was to find a square hole in which to fit? Has your natural intelligence been suppressed? Perhaps it's time to find out if you have hidden talents or another form of intelligence you would prefer to work with. In your notebook jot down your thoughts about multiple intelligences, which ones you believe you have and which you'd like to explore further.

Natural talents or learned skills?

Another word that could be used to describe any of the intelligences you are born with is "talent". Talents are something you are naturally good at without having to make much effort to develop. Skills are different as they require you to learn specific knowledge and apply that knowledge in a prescribed way. An example of a talent is the ability to look at a derelict house and visualize how it could appear if you were to completely renovate it. Skills that can translate the vision into reality include learning how to draw this mental image as an architectural drawing (giving details of the structure) and also graphic design (suggesting what it would look like visually in full color).

Anthony had a talent for working with numbers plus an ability to recognize patterns and trends. He went to college and learnt the skill of financial accounting. He also had the natural ability to explain complex rules in simple ways. Anthony now helps other people manage their personal and business finances effectively, not only by completing their accounts for them but advising them on how to structure their business for greater financial gain. As others appreciate what he does, Anthony gains a great sense of satisfaction. This role of serving others and supporting his family at the same time is a large part of Anthony living out his purpose in life. He combined a natural talent with a learned skill.

Fiona Harold calls these natural talents and learned skills "signature strengths". In her book *The Seven Rules of Success* she suggests, "Aligning your purpose with your signature strengths is the sure-fire route to personal fulfilment and a successful life." She continues by saying, "I'm convinced that each of us has a purpose and that our personal talents and individual circumstances throughout life present us with the opportunities to fulfil that purpose."

○○○○○○○○○○○○○○○○○○○○○○○○○○○○○○○○○○○○○○

EXERCISE: Listing your talents and strengths
Take a page in your notebook and divide it into two columns. At the top of one put the title "natural talents", at the top of the other put "learned skills". Now think back over your life and list your talents and skills under the appropriate columns. Does anything jump out at you? Don't worry if it doesn't. These lists will be useful for the following exercise.

○○○○○○○○○○○○○○○○○○○○○○○○○○○○○○○○○○○○○○

STEP 5: PLAY TO YOUR STRENGTHS

Find your X-factor

Every individual has a unique mix of talents and skills. Skills can be developed through formal study at college or university, informal learning through reading books or researching on the internet, coaching and mentoring at work, or by many other means. Combining your skills with your talents can result in a strength you can use to your advantage. You could call this combination your X-factor. It is easier to recognize your X-factor when:

- You are exceptionally gifted with a natural talent
- You have worked hard to develop a skill to a high level
- You are very passionate about your talent or skill

Here are a few examples of combining talents with skills to create new possibilities:

- Good with languages and people (talents) + qualified mechanic (skill):
  = Possibilities: teach mechanics in developing countries; translate manuals.

- Empathy for animals (talent) + project management and funding applications (skills):
  = Possibilities: set up a pet rescue centre; help animal charities get funding.

- Enjoy dancing, music and socializing (talents) + business studies graduate (skills):
  = Possibilities: create a dance studio; manage theatre productions.

○○

EXERCISE: Finding your X-factor
Look back over the list of talents and skills you've just identified. Try putting

them together in different combinations. What can you come up with? Can you see any new possibilities that would be worth exploring further?

○ ○

If you've discovered you have a distinct X-factor then I'd encourage you to consider the quote, "Only do what only you can do." If on the other hand you feel your X-factor isn't unique then be reassured, there's nothing to worry about. There are many who have talents and skills that are similar to yours. However, no one on this earth will share your unique personality. It's not just what you do that counts, it's also the way you do it. For example, a few years ago I changed both my hairdresser and my dentist. Was I attracted to them because I thought they were more competent than others? No, it was because I liked their friendly personalities and the way they treated me. Don't feel you have to start afresh and develop a new X-factor – though this might be right for some. And definitely don't live your life trying to become someone else. Instead, let your personality shine through and decide to be the best you that only you can be.

Uncover your hidden talents

What if you don't feel you have found your true talents yet? There could be a number of reasons why this is so. Perhaps you are unaware of how gifted you are – a common problem among creative people. Mick was one of those guys. He could sing, play 10 different instruments, record his playing through a mixer and create amazing new songs. He was literally a one-man band. When people would praise him for his brilliant creations he would typically reply, "What I do is simple, anyone could do it." He couldn't see that only the gifted few might ever get close to doing what he did. His talent was plain to see for everyone – but himself. Mick had a blind spot. If only he could have seen himself as others saw him he would have recognized his amazing potential.

STEP 5: PLAY TO YOUR STRENGTHS

Listening to what others say about you can provide you with clues. Do people praise you for what you do? This could be for something you consider to be part of normal everyday life such as cooking, homemaking, caring for family or helping to run a local group. What is it that they recognize and admire in you? What underlying talents do these skills rely upon? Also, why is it that people seek you out? Do you find yourself regularly being asked to help out in some way? Do people come to you for advice? What do others want to talk to you about? Could it be that they value your opinions on relationships, money, parenting, gardening or how to solve problems? If so, these might point towards talents undetected by you but clearly recognized by others.

○○○○○○○○○○○○○○○○○○○○○○○○○○○○○○○○○○○○○

EXERCISE: Uncovering hidden talents
Make a list of at least three but preferably five or more friends, family or work colleagues who know you well and you can trust. Ask them for honest feedback by saying, "Could you help me? I'm working through a book on life coaching and one exercise requires me to ask people I trust to tell me what they think my natural gifts and abilities are. What would you say they are?" Listen carefully for anything that stands out to you and thank them for their honesty.

○○○○○○○○○○○○○○○○○○○○○○○○○○○○○○○○○○○○○

Another problem you could have is that your life's experiences might be limited. Most people have not had the opportunity to explore all the different forms of intelligence that Gardner taught about. Have you learnt to play an instrument, become fluent in other languages, mastered a form of dancing, succeeded in a sport, created a work of art, served other people and done something good for the environment? If you have, great! You can reflect on all this and ask yourself what you found easiest and most enjoyable. Those things we master quickly and enjoy the most are often an expression of our natural talents. You may find it easier to work with these in future.

If you haven't had the opportunity to work with some of these forms of intelligence you may want to think about how you can explore them at this stage in life. If you've never played a musical instrument before ask a friend who does to show you some of the basics and let you have a go one evening. Then ask them for their honest feedback. If you find the piano difficult then why not try the guitar, or a clarinet, or the drums? Different instruments suit different people. How about art? Take a clean piece of paper and a sharp pencil and have a go at drawing something. Not tried out another language? Why not visit your local library and borrow one of their introductory audio language programmes? You're unlikely to become an expert immediately but within a short time you may discover something new you have a knack for. The important thing is to try out new things that give you the opportunity to explore other forms of intelligence that might reveal previously unrecognized talents.

The challenge of many talents

What if you find you are good at many things in life? This is a good problem to have, but a problem nonetheless. One option is to choose a single core talent and focus on it, such as working as a full-time dancer. A second is to find a way to combine and work with two or more talents at the same time, for example, if you can dance and teach why not become a dance instructor? A third is to focus on one talent now and refocus on others later. You could start out as a dancer, then become a dance instructor, and after developing business skills end up running a chain of dance studios. In retirement you may switch your attention to developing your artistic skills.

Josh is faced with a dilemma. He originally went to college to take A-levels but the academic approach didn't suit him so he transferred to a practical course in furniture making. Amazed at the progress Josh made, his tutor directed other students to him to learn the detailed marquetry techniques he skilfully mastered. But Josh also loves water

STEP 5: PLAY TO YOUR STRENGTHS

sports. A couple of years ago, aged 17, he was runner up in the UK surf-ski competition and he's beat an Olympic gold medallist in an international sea kayak race. Having succeeded in both water sports and making furniture he looked for a fresh challenge and has recently taken up ice-skating. Being gifted in several areas has made it difficult for Josh to choose one clear pathway forward. It will be interesting to see what he ends up doing.

If you have several talents, it may be possible to find a way to incorporate them together in life. Elisabeth, who founded The Donkey Sanctuary we mentioned earlier, clearly had naturalistic intelligence. She also discovered an interpersonal intelligence with a passion for supporting children with special needs and disabilities. This led her to set up a programme of activities providing donkey-assisted therapy for local schools and care centres.

Sometimes, working with one talent for your employment, such as teaching, and another for your recreational activity, such as art, might be a sensible way forward. Thinking about this, one option for Josh could be to work as a high quality furniture maker during the week and then enjoy being a semi-professional sportsperson at the weekends. Again, Steven and Judith Estrine have a comment that might be worth considering for those with more than one talent:

> *It might be wise to seek some of your satisfaction from hobbies and interests outside of work. In this way you can insulate yourself against the ups and downs of your working life. Viewing your job as a means of income generation to support the rest of life may be healthier than relying on it to make you continuously happy.*

Work in tune with your personality type

Some organizations place a lot of weight on understanding personality types. There are a number of psychometric profiling tools out there that you can use to help you understand what makes you tick and why you do things the way you do. Probably the most well known of these is the Myers-Briggs Type Indicator (MBTI). By answering a set of questions you can discover what kind of person you are. Your MBTI profile is based on four sets of opposite characteristics such as being extrovert or introvert. This gives rise to 16 different combinations.

Career coaches sometimes encourage you to take an MBTI test to help them understand what your preferences are and therefore what sort of work you may be best suited to. Paul D Tieger and Barbara Barron-Tieger co-authored a book on the subject called, *Do What You Are: Discover the Perfect Career for You Through the Secrets of Personality Type*. What they say makes a lot of sense. If you're an introverted, logical, analytical type you may struggle if you find yourself in a job that demands you to work in an extroverted manner, making snap decisions based on your intuition. As well as offering general guidance, their book goes into some depth in relation to each of the sixteen MBTI profiles. You can use this with their lists of MBTI-matched career options to help you explore alternative work that may suit you.

Don't imprison yourself by your past

Some people feel a pressure to keep doing what they've always done. But do you have to stick with your current path in life just because you are good at it? Not necessarily. While you may have been successful in one area of employment it doesn't mean you have to continue with it.

Emma completed her degree and feeling the pressure to earn money found a job in an accountant's office. She was very good at what she did and quickly gained promotion at work. Then one day she attended a personal effectiveness training event. Reflecting on her life, she recognized that she had chosen her current job out of necessity, not because it was the career she had wanted. Even though those around her considered Emma to be a model of success at work, deep down she knew she

STEP 5: PLAY TO YOUR STRENGTHS

wasn't doing what she really wanted to do with her life. To get back on track Emma decided to leave her current job and return to university to study law. Just because she was successful in one career didn't mean she had to stick with it. If you are feeling stale or frustrated in your current role then maybe it's time for you to pause and reflect. You also have the right to consider alternative options for your future.

Over the years I've had the opportunity to coach and train people who have taken personality profile assessments at various stages of their lives. Interestingly, some people seem to maintain their profile or personality type over a long period of time but others don't. Life's experiences and challenges have at times demanded that individuals take on new areas of responsibility. This can result in them developing new skills and can to some extent reshape their character. This often happens when people change careers, take up managerial positions, or take time out to care for family.

You may have started out with one personality profile in your younger years. However, through life's circumstances and your personal development you may now have an updated set of skills and preferences. Your profile can change. Being reshaped by your work or family environment is a reactive approach. However, you can also consciously choose to change your perceived profile.

Sanjeev was a shy, introverted and thoughtful type. When he saw that those who were being promoted at work were more extroverted and made decisions quickly he figured out that by changing his approach he could improve his chances of promotion. He made more effort to mix with others and started offering his opinions on issues at team meetings. He was soon noticed and given the promotion opportunity he sought. Interestingly, what at first felt unnatural soon became comfortable for him as he grew into the new role and way of working.

If you feel comfortable with your current personality profile then I'd encourage you to seek out opportunities or roles that harmonize with it. On the other hand, if you see a different type of work that requires you to function in a way that is outside your current comfort zone, don't dismiss it straight away. It could be an opportunity for you to set yourself free from your past and begin a new future. The barriers you perceive are more likely to be inside your head than outside in the world around you. You have permission and the freedom to choose a new pathway forward.

Before we leave this subject of being imprisoned by your past, it may help you to realize that you are not indispensible. A time will come when either voluntarily or otherwise you will be removed from your current role. At that point, someone else may take your place. This will give them the opportunity to develop. It could even be that they may do a better job than you. But even if they don't, seeing that others can come in and take your place can be liberating.

Gina had been helping out for some time in the Sunday School at her church. While the children seemed happy enough she felt an inner restlessness. For several years she had been developing her musical abilities and had a growing desire to play in the church music group – something she couldn't do with her current commitment. Gina couldn't see anyone else who could take over her role so felt trapped. It was only when one of the leaders asked for new volunteers that someone stepped forward, bringing with them a fresh enthusiasm for the children's work. Gina soon started playing regularly in the church group and after she moved for work went on to lead a group of her own in another church. But it would have never happened had she stayed in the role of Sunday School Teacher.

○○○○○○○○○○○○○○○○○○○○○○○○○○○○○○○○○○○○

EXERCISE: Alternative lives
To help you discover some new possibilities try out the following. Set aside 20 minutes and find a place where you won't be disturbed. You will need a notebook and pen. Describe in writing four alternative lives you could have lived, giving yourself five minutes to write each description. These could

STEP 5: PLAY TO YOUR STRENGTHS

relate to any time in history and any part of the world. You could be young or old, rich or poor, male or female. Don't worry if you don't manage to describe each life fully, you can always come back to them later. The purpose of the exercise is to get you to generate ideas without thinking through them too much in advance. Reflect on these alternative lives. What can you learn from them? How different are they to your current life? What patterns do you recognize? What excited you most when you were writing? Which one appeals to you the most? Why is this? Again, record any important insights in your notebook.

ooooooooooooooooooooooooooooooooooooooo

You can develop new strengths

You really can develop new strengths. I've proved this is possible. My first career was as a vehicle technician. It was something I was good at. Then I hurt my back and decided it was time to give up the heavy physical work. Not sure what to do next I went to a careers advisor and told them I was interested in becoming a teacher but needed to earn a salary from day one. They then asked me a few questions: "Do you have a teaching qualification?" I had to be honest so confessed, "No." "How about teaching experience?" "None." I replied. "Do you currently work with young people?" "Not really, I struggle to relate to them." The advisor looked puzzled but suggested taking a skills profiling test. "The results suggest that teaching is not a good match for you." Perhaps because I couldn't think of anything else to do, I went ahead and started looking for teaching opportunities anyway. One of the local colleges was advertising for part-time lecturers in automotive engineering. Within a few weeks I was standing in front of a room of eager young apprentices. My knees were knocking, my voice was trembling and I nearly wet myself. I progressed from teaching mechanics to teaching management and business studies. Over the next twenty years I gained a Masters Degree in Management Development, taught thousands of people, mostly managers and business owners, and developed a new strength.

You can develop new strengths too. Take Arnold Schwarzenegger as an example. He initially made a name for himself as a body-builder. Having achieved the titles of Mr Universe and Mr Olympia he subsequently ventured into acting. Following years of box-office hit films he retired from acting and moved into politics and held the post of Governor of California for seven years. Having stood down from this role, he has become increasingly engaged in philanthropic activities such as supporting after-school activities for young people. Along the way he has obviously learnt many lessons. One of these can be an encouragement for you if you want to try something new but are finding it challenging: "Strength does not come from winning. Your struggles develop your strengths. When you go through hardships and decide not to surrender, that is strength."

So, just because you don't have a track record of success in one area of life doesn't mean you can't be good at it in future. It may be that you have untapped talent that's just waiting to be released. Alternatively, you could work at developing a new skill in an area you've not tried before. Don't be put off if you don't seem to have a natural talent but yet still want to have a go at something. Many books on success suggest that it's not always the talented that succeed, rather it's those who persevere in working at what they're focusing on.

○○○

EXERCISE: Developing new strengths

You've thought about talents and skills that you already have. You've also asked others for their feedback to identify possible hidden talents. Now is the time to question whether there are any new strengths you would like to develop. As a starting point, look back over the chapter where we explored your dreams. Are there any dreams you identified where you felt you lacked the skills needed to pursue them? If so, what skills would be useful to you

STEP 5: PLAY TO YOUR STRENGTHS

if you were to pursue these dreams? Make a note of them in your notebook and consider whether you would like to find a way to test out and develop such skills.

○ ○

You can turn your weaknesses into strengths

Though most books on success would play this down as a strategy, this could still be another way forward for some people. One famous American football player and coach, Knute Rockne, gave the following advice to those he coached: "Build up your weaknesses until they become your strong points." Recognizing that your weaknesses can cause your downfall and then consciously choosing to do something about them can make you more effective as a person. Triscia runs a business that employs a handful of staff. She struggled to understand the financial side of her business activities so enrolled on an accountancy course. After two years of part-time study she reached the point where she knew more than her accountant when it came to managing her business finances. She then dismissed her first accountant and found another she could work with. Together they looked at how they could restructure the business, save thousands in tax and make more profit. Triscia had turned her weakness into a strength.

Jane suffers from a partial hearing loss problem. Because of this, she has learnt to lip-read and is able to see what people are saying. Also, because she depends on what her eyes tell her more than the average person, she's developed the ability to read body language. This is a great strength when working with individuals and small groups as she does. Jane hasn't let her weakness stop her, but has used it as a trigger to develop new strengths.

And have you heard of Oscar Pistorius from South Africa? As a baby suffering from a congenital birth defect he had both legs amputated below the knees. With two prosthetic limbs it's a huge challenge just to learn to walk well. As he grew, Oscar wanted to play sports like normal children. Having struggled with rugby he wondered what it would be like to run. With specially designed artificial limbs his dream came true and he took up running. In the 2012 London Paralympics, aged 25, he set a new world record and won the gold medal for the 400 metre race. Having no legs hasn't stopped Oscar from running nor from competing at the highest level of the sport. He has turned what most would see as his greatest weakness into his greatest strength.

Pause for a moment and reflect: do you recognize any weaknesses in your own life? Instead of ignoring them, can you use them to your advantage? Try this simple six-step approach to convert your weaknesses into strengths:

1. Identify and honestly admit your weaknesses

2. Choose which weaknesses to work on and in which order

3. Visualize yourself having made progress in converting the weakness into a strength

4. Set yourself small but achievable steps to work towards

5. Positively affirm your emerging strength aloud by saying, "Every day I am getting better at [your developing strength]"

6. Make a conscious effort to exercise your new strength every day

Don't get discouraged and don't give up. It usually takes about six weeks of persistent effort before you notice a measurable change. Encourage yourself by memorising this little saying:

Sow a thought, reap an act.
Sow an act, reap a habit.
Sow a habit, reap a character.
Sow a character, reap a destiny.

STEP 5: PLAY TO YOUR STRENGTHS

Turn adversity into opportunity

If you've been through tough times you may be able to turn it to your advantage. Many people who've suffered hardships and difficulties have learnt so much that they now have something useful to share with others. Karim Jaude built a multi-million dollar business in his home country of Lebanon. Then he was kidnapped and forced to give his wealth over to his captors. After being released he fled to Iran and built a new business. Three years later he was forced to flee for his life and ended up in America. Again, starting from scratch he built yet another property-based business. He now teaches others how to build a profitable property business from the ground up. Reflecting on his own experience of adversity Karim says: "Always remember that adversity is a call to action. Getting knocked down doesn't count, getting back up does. It is not what happens to you that matters, it is how you react to it and what you do with it that matters."

Many have testified that adversity has been a training ground that has developed both perseverance and character. As we just heard Arnold Schwarzenegger say, "Your struggles develop your strengths." In the opening line of his best-selling book, *The Road Less Travelled*, M Scott Peck says, "Life is difficult." He goes on to explain that the struggle is probably more to do with the way we see things rather than life itself. By accepting the truth that life is difficult and we are likely to face challenges we empower ourselves to overcome the difficulties. We can set ourselves free from the power of the fear of suffering and the illusion that life should be easy for us all the time. We recognize courage when we see someone pressing forwards into the face of fear. We observe patience when we watch a person who struggles with ongoing suffering. As difficult as it may be, adversity is a fertile field in which to grow character.

There are situations when the right thing to do with adversity is to struggle and push against it. Nearly two hundred years ago a group of about thirty tradesmen, frustrated at having to pay high prices for poor quality goods, believed they could create a better social order. Pooling their resources, they sought to sell food and other produce at a price their members and customers could afford. Founded on clearly defined principles that fought against discrimination and for democracy, they set up The Rochdale Society of Equitable Pioneers. The business model they created formed the basis of what we call the co-operative movement that today supports an estimated one billion members and 100 million jobs worldwide. Co-operative working helps promote fair trade, provides employment, reduces poverty and strengthens communities.

Then there are other occasions when it may be wiser to embrace adversity and continue with life knowing you can never run from it. Sometimes it's possible that if you accept adversity you can transform it into a purposeful opportunity. Perhaps one of the most extraordinary examples I've come across of someone coming to terms with adversity and going on to do something purposeful with his life is Nick Vujicic. Born without arms or legs, Nick found life tough. He relied on his younger brother to do almost everything for him. Being bullied at school, he contemplated suicide. Then he read an article about someone else who was struggling with a severe disability. Nick made a decision to embrace his own situation and make the most of life. With some help, he learned to use the stump and two toes where a leg should be to write, use a computer, brush his teeth and many other daily tasks the rest of us take for granted. Wanting to help and inspire others, he set up a non-profit organization called Life Without Limbs. Nick now travels the world and has spoken to more than three million people in more than 24 countries. A lot of his motivational speaking focuses on inspiring and encouraging teenagers. He's also written a book, *Life Without Limits: Inspiration for a Ridiculously Good Life*. If you want to learn more about how this one young man turned adversity into an opportunity then get a copy of his book or check out his website.

STEP 5: PLAY TO YOUR STRENGTHS

EXERCISE: Transforming adversity into opportunity
Have you been through a period of adversity? What did you learn from it? Can you use what you learnt to help others facing similar challenges? If you're still facing some form of adversity, can you see how you can grow through it? How might you be able to turn this to your advantage or use it for the benefit of others?

> **Key thoughts to take away:**
>
> We all have natural talents and we can all develop new skills. We each face different circumstances in life that present us with unique opportunities. Working with our strengths is the surest way to find success. Key thoughts to take away from this chapter include:
>
> - You are more intelligent than you thought you were
> - You can find your X-factor
> - You can uncover hidden talents
> - You don't have to keep doing what you've always done
> - You can develop new strengths
> - You can turn weakness into strength
> - You can transform adversity into opportunity
> - Be the best you that only you can be
>
> So far this book has encouraged you to do a lot of reflection, thinking about your strengths, dreams, inner guidance system

and doing something worthwhile. It's now time to pull all these things together and plan your way forward from here. That's what the next chapter will help you to do.

o o o

STEP 6:
PLAN YOUR WAY FORWARD

RE-ALIGN YOUR LIFE WITH YOUR PURPOSE

ooo

STEP 6
Plan Your Way Forward
Re-align Your Life with Your Purpose

○ ○ ○

"Decide upon your major definite purpose in life and then organize all your activities around it."
(Brian Tracy – personal development speaker)

○ ○ ○

Pulling the pieces together

LIFE HAD BECOME STALE FOR SAM. Though she was successful in her role as a senior administrator, the job no longer provided the excitement it once had. Then she had a life-threatening health scare that made her stop and think. What was she doing with her life? If she were to die shortly, what legacy would she leave? Thankfully, following surgery, her health improved. Something else also changed for the better. Sam came away from the experience with a desire to do something more meaningful with her life. Having survived her ordeal she wanted to give hope and encouragement to other women who faced similar health issues. Noticing that her openness and honesty in discussing her condition had helped friends and family, the thought struck her that many more could benefit from her experience were she to write a book. She returned to college and having completed a part-time writing course she is now close to finishing her book. Though her health scare has possibly been the biggest challenge she ever experienced in life, it has also led Sam to do something that has given her a huge sense of personal fulfilment. Sam's hope is that through her efforts thousands of other women will also receive encouragement as they read her story in future.

STEP 6: PLAN YOUR WAY FORWARD

Sam managed to pull all the pieces together. Following her health scare Sam gained a clearer perspective on life. Then she thought seriously about doing something more worthwhile with her time. Reflecting on her personal values and inner motivation, she recognized a desire to serve others and express herself creatively. This helped to bring into focus a dream that had lain dormant in her life until now, to write a book. Though she knew she had a natural ability to communicate effectively, Sam knew she needed to develop the skill of writing a book. By developing her strengths, she formulated a plan to fulfil her personal vision. The result? Her book should be published next year, other women will be given hope and encouragement, and for Sam, she is now living a happier and more fulfilled life.

Do you recognize the steps we've covered so far in this book? We've looked at perspective, doing something worthwhile, inner guidance, dreams and strengths. If you've worked through the exercises you should have a much clearer picture of these by now. The next step is to pull them together and come up with a plan.

Donna's got a passion; to help women look young and beautiful, naturally. Having rejuvenated the appearance of many women through facial massage treatments, she became concerned about the cosmetics they were using. As well as the ethical considerations surrounding the development and testing of beauty products, she learnt about the effects that chemicals could have on the body. But what could she do? Rather than attack the giants in the cosmetics industry she decided to take a different approach by preparing to open a shop selling natural cosmetics. To do so she needed a plan, so Donna enrolled on a business-planning course for women entrepreneurs. The course helped her think through her ideas, prompting her to find the right people to talk to and enabling her to develop a sound plan from which she could launch her new business. It's early days for Donna but the first signs are that other women are waking up to the idea that natural cosmetics can look just as good but are far less damaging to their skin.

To help Donna come up with a plan she was asked to look at a number of things. First, she needed to be clear about the reason why she wanted to do what she wanted to do. Next, she was questioned about how big she thought her business might become. After considering her personal readiness for such a venture, she then estimated the financial projections and implications. This led her to take action and talk to a team of financial and legal experts who helped her move to the next stage of her planning. Though you may not be thinking of starting your own business at this stage, applying some of these principles to your own situation can still help you if you're looking to head off in a new direction.

Take responsibility for your life

I find it fascinating to learn about people who have become successful in life. Some come from privileged upbringings where prosperity was handed to them on a plate; others come from deprived backgrounds and had to work hard to achieve success. At one end of the scale you have royalty and nobility who are born into wealth. At the other you have people like Tony Robbins, the American self-help author and motivational speaker, who confessed to living in a low rent apartment for some time. Then there's Robert Kiyosaki, the very successful businessman, educator and author of the *Rich Dad, Poor Dad* series of books, who was homeless and lived out of his car at one stage earlier on in his career.

Just because you come from humble origins doesn't mean you have less opportunity to find a way forward than those who come from more privileged positions. The difference that makes the difference is your mindset. If you believe you are a victim of your circumstances then you will not make the effort to change your life for the better. Choosing to think differently opens up opportunities. Believing something is possible is half the battle towards making it reality.

There are times when we need to take our eyes off our circumstances, stop looking back to past failures, push our fears to one side

STEP 6: PLAN YOUR WAY FORWARD

and choose to move forward with hope and confidence. Judith Leary-Joyce, author of *The Psychology of Success* wrote, "The moment you take responsibility for your life is the moment you take off. Life really is what we make of it and it is up to you whether you make it good or bad." Both Tony Robbins and Robert Kiyosaki took responsibility for their lives and turned them around completely. If you listen to either of them for long you will hear that this is one of their key messages; you too need to take responsibility for your life.

Sometimes circumstances happen that challenge you to face up to life. If you are confronted by redundancy, ill heath, bereavement, debt or some other crisis, no doubt you get the feeling you need to respond in some way. There may be opportunities that come your way unexpectedly through a chance meeting, an idea popping into your head, or a surge of people seeking you out for your expertise. Or you might just decide that now is the time to do something different, to fulfil a long-term desire or to start your own business. Whatever the trigger, the key is to take responsibility for your own future. Taking responsibility means recognizing you have the ability to choose how you will respond in life.

○ ○

EXERCISE: Taking responsibility for your life

Are you taking full responsibility for your life? Or are you blaming circumstances for where you are now? Are you taking responsibility for every area of your life? For your health and fitness? For your psychological and emotional wholeness? For your financial well-being? For your future? If you realize you're not taking full response-ability for an area of life, admit it, face up to it and choose to do something about it. You may even want to make a note in your notebook or repeat out loud, "From now on, I take full responsibility for my life and my future. In particular, I take full response-ability for [name those areas that are important for you]."

○ ○

Work out what you don't want

Many life coaches are trained to ask their clients what it is they would like to do, then they find ways to help them achieve their stated goals. If you're not completely sure what it is that you want, try a different starting point that may prove helpful. Try asking yourself what it is that you don't like about life as it stands. Working out what you don't want to do can be just as revealing – and is sometimes easier to pinpoint.

John and Laura lived in the suburbs of a major city. John worked as a manager and Laura as a senior administrator, both in well-respected large companies. Shortly before the birth of their first child they asked themselves what they liked and disliked about life as they contemplated their future. The downsides they wanted to eliminate included the frustratingly slow and congested commute, air pollution, the general hustle and bustle of city life, the rising crime rate and living with the threat of potential redundancy. Knowing what they didn't want in life helped guide towards what they did. Within a few short months, John found himself another job in a small town several hundred miles away. Selling their house, they relocated to a quiet village only minutes from the coast. The frustrations of being trapped in traffic jams were replaced by peaceful drives down free-flowing country roads. The commute that sometimes took up to an hour each way now dropped to less than fifteen minutes. City smog was replaced by a clear, coastal breeze and when visiting the local town, John and Laura could stroll leisurely along rather than having to weave their way through the busy crowds like they used to.

Life does not have to continue to be how it always has been. You have permission to review and change your life. Sure, there are always consequences to your decisions and it's wise to try to think about them. After moving, John and Laura found that living near the coast meant they saw more rain. They also didn't have such a wide range of shops to visit in the local town. And maybe in future there may not be as many career opportunities close by. But they soon discovered they were not on their own. They began to meet many others who had fled the busy life of the city for a quiet life in the country. One thing they found they had in common was a desire to improve their quality of life rather than just increase their quantity in life. John and Laura worked out what they didn't want, which led them to identify what they did want. Then they took responsibility, took action, and made their dream come true.

○○○○○○○○○○○○○○○○○○○○○○○○○○○○○○○○○○○○○○

EXERCISE: Working out what you don't want
Take stock of your life right now. Is there anything you don't like about it? Is there anything that's part of your daily life that you really don't want and you would like to change? If so, what's the opposite of it? How could you change your life so you have less of what you don't want and more of what you do?

○○○○○○○○○○○○○○○○○○○○○○○○○○○○○○○○○○○○○○

Be proactive

My guess is that by this stage you may be experiencing a range of feelings. I'd hope you can appreciate your strengths more fully, see your dream more clearly, and work out what's more worthwhile to do with your life. However, you could also recognize that there may be some things you'd like to change about life and you may feel challenged to take greater responsibility for your future. If you want a better future tomorrow you need to make a proactive decision today. In his book *The Seven Habits of Highly Effective People*, Stephen Covey says the number one habit is to be proactive; effective people consciously choose to take responsibility for their own lives and their future. They then do something about it.

Remember Emma who I mentioned a little earlier? Within the personal effectiveness training event she was encouraged to become more proactive. After thinking through her priorities it dawned on her that she was heading in the wrong direction. She had settled into a comfortable job that paid a fair wage but didn't stretch her as a person. She knew she was capable of more and realized that instead of getting into the groove at work she was stuck in a rut. That's when she chose to be proactive and reset the direction of her life. Securing a place on a law degree at university, she handed in her notice. Emma took responsibility, took action and created a better future for herself.

Being proactive doesn't mean having a detailed plan of how you intend to change life, it means choosing to take responsibility with the intention of developing a plan. But I want you to see that proactivity is more than just making a singular decision, it's an ongoing attitude, a way of living. By making a conscious choice to become proactive in the first place you empower yourself to rise above your circumstances and create a better life for yourself. By remaining proactive you maintain your position on top of your circumstances.

Ask yourself the right questions

Taking responsibility and deciding to be proactive is a conscious choice. It's as if a conversation takes place within yourself about how you are going to move on from where you are at. I've met a few people who have told me, "I gave myself a stiff talking to." As a child at school there was a saying that the first sign of madness is talking to yourself. As I've grown older and read many books on psychology and self-development I now believe the opposite to be true. Talking to yourself is a sign of sanity. It shows that you know where you are at in life and can draw upon your own wisdom to both challenge and guide you. Sometimes I say aloud, "Mervyn, you need to do something about this!" As I hear myself I know what I'm saying is true and it prompts me to take action. There are other times when instead of making a statement I ask myself questions. "Mervyn, what are you going to do about this?" Asking

STEP 6: PLAN YOUR WAY FORWARD

yourself questions is a powerful way of finding new ways forward in life. The skill is to ask yourself the right questions.

Keith Cameron Smith decided it was time to improve his financial situation. He knew there were many who were much wealthier than he was and thought there must be some secret, some hidden knowledge that they had found that he hadn't. He asked himself, "Keith, how is it that these people have more money than you? And how are you going to improve your own financial position?" He promised himself that he would find out what it was that they knew but he didn't. So he got in touch with a number of millionaires and asked if he could interview them. From his findings he noticed patterns of thought and action that these richer-than-average people shared. With a bit more effort he managed to rank them in some order of importance. As a consequence he ended up publishing a book titled, *The Top 10 Habits Of Millionaires*.

What do you think was the most powerful habit that millionaires shared that other less wealthy people didn't? Was it that they were more ruthless and aggressive in their business dealings? No. How about luck? Did many of them inherit wealth from their family? Wrong again. The one thing that stood out above all others was that they asked themselves empowering questions. That means they had learned to look at life differently and chose to find a way forward, believing that they could make things work out for the better. For example, you could ask yourself the question, "Can I make a million dollars in the next five years?" That's a fair question and well worth pondering. You're likely to come to the conclusion that you have a choice of answers: yes, no or maybe. According to Smith, millionaires just add one tiny three-letter word to change the whole situation and guarantee success. Instead, they use what some would call possibility thinking. The question they would ask is, "How can I make a million dollars in the next five years?"

Do you see the difference? They've already worked out what it is they want to achieve. They tell themselves it's possible then they challenge themselves to find a way to turn possibility into reality. Likewise, when you are contemplating the way forward it will help you to ask yourself the right questions. Try adding that simple yet powerful word to turn your situation around. Ask yourself questions like, "How can I make this work? How can I achieve my dream? How can I move from doing what I'm doing now to what I want to do in future?"

By the way, having heard Keith speaking at a business conference there was something he said I feel is important to add at this stage. He encouraged all of us to aim to become millionaires – but not for the money itself, not for what that money could buy. No, he noticed that those who had become wealthy had learnt so much about life, themselves and other people along the way. They had grown and matured as people. It seems as if their journey through life had been enriched more by the personal qualities they developed than the cash they accumulated.

○○

EXERCISE: Ask yourself empowering questions
If you've not done so before, start asking yourself empowering questions. Add that little word that makes all the difference. Start asking yourself "How?" Try it at the beginning of the day, "How can I make best use of this day?" Try it at the end of the day, "How can I make my dream a reality?" Let your subconscious work on it overnight. Try it throughout the day. Make up your own empowering questions.

○○

Focus on your priorities

In Stephen Covey's book *First Things First* he emphasizes the importance of having clearly identified priorities. One memorable quote of his that many others repeat is, "The main thing is to keep the main thing the main thing." This assumes you've worked out what really is the main thing in your life. To do so, you need to tap into your inner

STEP 6: PLAN YOUR WAY FORWARD

guidance system. What are your core values? What motivates you the most? What is your conscience telling you?

Covey talks much about the difference between living a reactive life and a proactive life. He advocates living according to your inward principles more than the outward demands that command your attention. To help you understand the tension between the two and to work out what is more important in life he says:

> *Our struggle to put first things first can be characterized by the contrast between two powerful tools that direct us: the clock and the compass. The clock represents our commitments, appointments, schedules, goals, activities – what we do with, and how we manage our time. The compass represents our vision, values, principles, mission, conscience, direction – what we feel is important and how we lead our lives.*

To get your priorities in order you need to live by the compass first, then look to the clock after. You should already be aware of your personal values, your principles and your conscience from working through step three. Your dreams from step four give you a direction to focus upon. In a moment we'll explore your thoughts on your personal mission and vision in life. Before we do that though, it will pay to think a bit more about priorities in general.

Some people focus on a single priority more than anything else. When I was young and single I raced motorcycles. My evenings and weekends were filled with fitness training, race bike preparation and the racing itself. Racing was my first priority, my second and my third. Everything else came in at position four or below. By being focused I ended up winning a championship. Now I'm older, have a wife, two children, and hopefully a bit more wisdom, my priorities have changed. My first priority is to live my life in accordance with my personal values, principles and beliefs. If I fail to do that I will be of no use either to myself or anyone else. Alongside that, my next priority is to care for my family. My commitment to doing purposeful work comes in third. If I don't do purposeful work I'm living in opposition to my core values and may fail in my duty to provide for my family. Everything else sits much further down the list.

Once you've worked out what's most important to you and you make your daily decisions in life based on your priorities, you will have more inner peace and you will achieve the outcomes that matter more to you. If you have several priorities in life then it's important to make sure they complement each other. With a single priority the key word is focus; with multiple priorities two words to hold onto are harmony and balance. For example, there may be times when my children may want my attention but I know I need to be working to provide financially for them. There are other times when I have plenty of work to do but I know it's better to take time out to be with my family. Being able to listen to my inner conscience and acting in line with my values helps me maintain the needed balance. I don't claim to have mastered this totally yet, but I believe I'm making progress. I've recognized the truth contained in a line quoted by Goethe the German poet: "Things which matter most must never be at the mercy of things which matter least."

○○○○○○○○○○○○○○○○○○○○○○○○○○○○○○○○○○○○○○○

EXERCISE: Clarifying your priorities
Look back at the exercises you previously completed where you identified your core values and thought about your dreams. What really is important to you? Again, if you had less than a year left in life, what would you want to give your time to? Alternatively, if you knew you had another twenty years of active life left, what would you want to achieve? Try writing these aims down in a list. Next, compare one against the other. Which is the most important on the list? And second most important? What about third?

○○○○○○○○○○○○○○○○○○○○○○○○○○○○○○○○○○○○○○○

Define your mission

Many businesses and other organizations have mission statements. Their purpose is to give direction to staff. They explain why the organization

STEP 6: PLAN YOUR WAY FORWARD

exists in the first place. It's the launch pad from which all business activity should take off. The mission statement should be the foundation for motivation. Remember when we discussed doing something worthwhile and I gave you the example of the company that made glass tubes? Their mission was to save lives of very young children. That's what motivated the staff. As we've said already, Google's stated mission is to "organize the world's information and make it easily accessible". I think they're doing a pretty good job of that so far. Knowing their mission keeps them focused and helps them add value for millions of people worldwide.

Likewise, as an individual, you can have your own personal mission statement. Your mission might not sound as grand as Google's but it is no less important. Being able to sum up your reason for being in one sentence is a powerful tool. If someone was to ask you, "What's your purpose in life?" can you give them a concise answer? The aim of being able to respond quickly and clearly is not to impress others but to show humbly that you know why you're here and what you're aiming to do with your life.

Whereas some people instinctively have a feel for what their mission in life is, others may need a little help in articulating this. Based on what we've covered so far in this book, here's one method for crafting your personal mission statement:

- First: Reflect on the strengths you identified within Step 5. Which would you like to work with most? Identify one or two from your list.

- Second: Review the values you identified in Step 3. List one or two that are most important to you.

- Third: Look back to Step 2 where you decided upon what was worthwhile and what you could give your life to. Try to sum this up in a short phrase.

- Fourth: Try combining the above in to a single sentence using the following template:

"My mission is to use my ability to [strengths identified] in line with my values of [values identified] to [do what you believe is worthwhile]."

- One example could be:

"My mission is to use my ability to build a business in line with my values of helping the poor in my city to start and run a social enterprise that provides essentials to the most needy in society."

- And another is:

"My mission is to use my abilities to teach others and communicate with people of different cultures in line with my values of empathy and service to help run a health education programme for young people in Africa."

- For those with family commitments another could be:

"My mission is first and foremost to support my family and then in my spare time to use my ability to relate to young people in line with my values of living an honest and helpful life to support the leaders and activities at the local youth club."

Try it for yourself. Make sure your mission statement is positive, describes your reason for being, is forward-looking and can be used to guide you in your everyday thinking, planning and decision-making. Make it the reference point against which you can judge all of your intended actions in life. It should be the driving force for all your activity. As Jack Canfield says, "Everything you do should be an expression of your purpose."

Focus on your vision

Your mission gives you your starting point. Your vision gives you your finishing point. Mission is the motivator that pushes you out of your starting blocks; vision is the power that pulls you towards the finishing line. It describes what you're aiming at. It's future focused and paints a picture of what you are trying to create.

STEP 6: PLAN YOUR WAY FORWARD

In a previous exercise you mapped out your journey to date and noted highs and lows, fast routes and slow, junctions and lay-bys. With your vision you will be looking over the horizon to where your journey will take you. If you were to add to your previous work and continue your journey, where will you end up? Where do you want to get to ultimately and what will life be like when you reach your final destination?

Generally, the clearer the vision is in your mind the stronger will be your motivation. Martin Luther King Jr had a vision of a country that was free from prejudice and injustice. It was so clear it not only inspired him but also those who heard him talk about it. His vision was also so big it could only be accomplished through the combined efforts of many people. He may have been the leader but his vision needed followers to join with him in supporting the cause to bring it into being. Your vision could start small and grow over time. Mother Teresa's vision was initially to relieve the suffering of a few people in India; it ended up becoming a vision that touched the lives of millions across the globe.

Some people create vision statements. Examples from larger organizations include: "To make people happy" (The Walt Disney Corporation) and "A world where everyone has a decent place to live" (Habitat for Humanity). A slightly more unusual but still very striking vision statement I came across is: "Wetlands sufficient to fill the skies with waterfowl today, tomorrow and forever" (Ducks Unlimited). If you are able to sum up your personal vision in a similar statement then it would definitely be worth writing down. Remember though to keep it brief, aspirational, visual and memorable.

Another way of capturing and communicating a vision for yourself is to create a vision board. This is a very visual tool that continually reminds you of your vision. To make a vision board find pictures, images, newspaper headlines or anything else that represents your future vision. Pin them up on a notice board somewhere where you can look at it regularly. This could be in your kitchen, bedroom, beside your desk or anywhere else you go regularly where you can pause and consider it from time to time. If you come across new images or headlines that fit with your vision then capture them also and add them to your vision board. I read of one man who cut out a picture of his ideal home from a magazine and within a few years ended up buying that very same house! Vision boards can be powerful.

Another powerful tool for preparing to outwork your purpose and achieve your aim is to practice visualization. To do this, close your eyes and picture yourself as having reached your goal in your own mind. Try to engage all your senses. What can you see? What can you hear? What does it feel like? Try to find a quiet place and time where you won't be disturbed then take a few minutes to explore your vision. Some psychologists say that repeated visualization helps to train the mind to find a way to bring your vision into being. Good times to practice visualization are first thing in the morning and last thing before you go to sleep. This is because these are the times when there is a transition between the conscious and the subconscious parts of your brain being in control. Visualising at that point enables you to transfer thoughts from your conscious mind to your subconscious more easily. As a result, your mind keeps mulling over your vision without you having to put a lot of effort into it.

Get SMART about your objectives

Once you've clarified your underlying mission and have a clear vision for the future, it's time to sharpen your focus. Having spent many years training others to succeed in the world of work, one of the simplest yet most powerful tools I taught was to set SMART objectives. This simply means getting really clear on what it is you're wanting to achieve. There's a saying that if you aim at nothing you're sure to hit it. SMART objectives make it very clear what you're aiming at, not only for you but anyone else who is interested. If you've not come across this idea before I'll just take a moment to explain what SMART stands for:

STEP 6: PLAN YOUR WAY FORWARD

- S = Specific – being able to describe exactly what it is you're focusing on
- M = Measurable – quantifying how much you expect to achieve
- A = Achievable – you've got to believe you can do it else you won't try
- R = Relevant – seeing how it benefits you provides the motivation
- T = Time-bound – you set yourself a deadline for achieving it

If you applied this to making money, you could tell yourself, "I'm going to make a million dollars then I'll retire." That sounds appealing – but it isn't SMART. It's an aspiration but it's too vague. If I re-wrote it as a SMART objective it would look a bit more like this: "I'm going to launch a new business selling clothes, making a $10,000 profit in year one and doubling that profit every year for the next seven years." Can you see how this meets the guidelines for SMART? Sure, you could be a bit more specific about what sort of clothes you're selling, and to who. But this could all be developed in your business plan. By the way, at the end of seven years you would have made more than one million dollars in profit – which could easily finance your retirement.

You could say aims or goals are generalizations, objectives are more specific. If you set yourself SMART objectives you will be able to measure your progress against them and know when you have achieved them. You could set yourself a range of objectives that relate to different areas of life. This can help you focus on maintaining a balance. You could have one for time spent with your family each week, another for an exercise program you will commit to this year, and another for what you want to achieve in your work in the next decade. You can also set SMART objectives in relation to your life purpose. Again, Jack Canfield has something to say about this. "Once you know your life purpose, determine your vision, and clarify what your true needs and desires are, you have to convert them into specific, measurable goals and objectives and then act on them with the certainty that you will achieve them."

○○○○○○○○○○○○○○○○○○○○○○○○○○○○○○○○○○○○○

EXERCISE: Setting SMART objectives
Reflect on your mission statement and your personal vision for the future. Identify a measurable outcome that would demonstrate you have achieved it at some point in future. At what point in time would you expect to reach your goal? Check that you believe this is something you can achieve. Now put it all together in one sentence. For example: "Within the next two years I will establish a social enterprise collecting and distributing surplus furniture that will make a profit which will be donated to the Children in Need charity." (Once established, you could then update your objective with a specific targeted amount to give each year.)

○○○○○○○○○○○○○○○○○○○○○○○○○○○○○○○○○○○○○

Consider practicalities

When it comes to planning your way forward in life there are three P's that are worth bearing in mind:

1. Be purposeful – do what you believe is worthwhile

2. Be passionate – do what you enjoy, but also

3. Be practical – find a way to cover your expenses in life

If you choose a pathway you are passionate about at the moment but you question whether what you're doing is worthwhile, it's likely that you could lose your enthusiasm and look for something else to do at some stage. Alternatively, if you take on a role that you believe is worthwhile but don't enjoy you can become discouraged and give up. I've known people give their lives in service for others because they felt it was what they ought to do only to find they were like a

STEP 6: PLAN YOUR WAY FORWARD

square peg in a round hole. They were doing good but their heart wasn't fully in it. By stepping out of the role and taking time to clarify their values and identify their strengths they were then able to seek a more appropriate shaped hole into which they could fit. I've also met people who found something they knew was worthwhile and were passionate about but then struggled because they were relying on it to provide an income to support themselves when it never would. They had to face up to the reality and be practical about their level of financial needs.

Some are in the privileged position of not needing to generate an income from their work. If that's you, great! Pursue your passion with zeal. However, if you are like the majority of people, you may need to find a way to survive financially. Don't be put off immediately though, do you remember the number one habit of millionaires? Don't ask yourself, "Can I afford to do this?" Instead, ask, "How can I afford to do this?" It's much more empowering.

Work out what you need to pay all your bills. Financial advisors would suggest you create a budget and make sure you live within your means. A starting point is to work out your survival budget – how much income you require to meet your basic needs. Generally, this includes food, accommodation, clothing and some would say pension provision. After that, identify your ideal budget – income required to meet your basic needs plus additional wants. Such wants can include holidays, entertainment, dining out and anything else you could survive without if you had to. A simple guideline for becoming wealthy is to spend less than you earn. I've also seen several advisors suggest you follow the 70/10/10/10 rule. This means to spend no more than 70% of what you earn on meeting your needs and wants, save 10% for the future, invest 10% in speculative ventures (but get proper advice before doing so) and give 10% away to good causes. That's great advice if you're able to do so but if you're not there yet it might be something to work towards.

Other practical advice if you're considering a major life change would be to aim to get out of debt, consider downsizing, and if you're looking to start a business venture then explore a range of financing options. If you are contemplating any significant investment of time or money I'd encourage you to talk it over with your nearest and dearest. One of the top three reasons people end up getting divorced is because of financial pressures in the relationship. I wouldn't want to see you succeed in business but fail in a relationship.

Over the years I've been asked to look at dozens of business plans when people have decided they want to launch out on their own in a new venture. I've been happy to take a look and give them my views as an impartial observer. However, I make no claim to be a financial advisor and I always strongly suggest that if you're thinking of setting up a new business then you need to do your research and get proper financial guidance.

When talking about dreams, aspirations and visions the focus is on what can be achieved. I believe this must be your starting point. However, before you take a leap into the dark I'd also suggest you take a bit of time out to test the viability of your idea, do some market research and some risk analysis. I remember one woman coming to me with a great idea for an environmentally friendly business. We then sat down and looked at the potential level of demand, clarified the total costs of doing what she wanted to do, then compared it with the price she could sell the recycled items for. Having done so, she could then see she wouldn't be able to make a profit from her proposed venture. It's then she realized why no-one else was already doing it. Risk analysis means simply asking what could go wrong, how bad could it be, and what could you do to prevent or manage it. When I was younger I used to get frustrated with people who would point out potential pitfalls. I now appreciate their contribution in helping me to see things I may have missed. Keep focused on your vision, but please, if you're starting a new venture, try to go in with your eyes wide open.

STEP 6: PLAN YOUR WAY FORWARD

EXERCISE: Considering the practicalities
If you've not already done so, work out your living costs. How much income do you need to meet your needs, and your wants? If you're planning a new venture, make a business plan and work out your sales, profit and cash flow forecasts. Do some risk analysis to make sure you've thought about what could go wrong and how you would cope if it did. Also, don't just think about the finance, how would pursuing your intended course of action affect those around you? Think through and talk through the practicalities with your partner, spouse, professional advisors or a trusted friend.

Plan your way forward

Stephen Covey's second of the seven habits of highly effective people is to "start with the end in mind". He suggests you need a clear picture of where you want to get to before you set off. This makes sense. If you want to head north there's no point in picking a road at random and then finding later that you're heading south. By having a clear vision that fits with your dream you have an end in mind. With SMART objectives written down you are even more focused on what you're hoping to achieve. The next step is to plan your route from where you are to where you want to be.

One approach to planning is to start from where you are at and work forwards. Ask yourself questions such as, "What can I do today, this week, this month, this year to move me closer to my goal?" You're likely to set short and medium-term goals that appear realistic and that you can work towards. This is a logical and safe approach that works for most people. If you're an optimistic person beware though, I've found there is some truth in the saying, "Most people overestimate what they can achieve in one year and underestimate what they could achieve in ten." Don't get too discouraged if you don't do all that you'd hoped to do, as long as you're making progress keep pressing forwards and you'll get there in the end.

If you have a big vision or huge ambition then there may be another way you could approach your planning. This time, start at the finishing line and work backwards. Visualize yourself as having arrived at your goal and achieved your vision. Write a statement as a declaration of having achieved your SMART objective. For example, "Within the past three years I have set up a charity, built a team and together we have funded the installation of 500 fresh water pumps for remote villages in Africa." Now ask yourself, "How did I get here, what was the previous step that led up to this?" Remember to start at the end and work backwards. Your plan could end up looking like this:

1. 500 pumps installed

2. 500 sites identified

3. 500 pumps purchased

4. Funding raised for 500 pumps

5. Promotional campaign rolled out

6. Promotional campaign planned and sponsors engaged

7. Registered charity set up and team recruited

You now have a clear plan of action. Where you have a completion date in mind you can then assign target dates for the completion of each stage. This approach works well when you have a clear vision of where you want to get to but aren't sure how to get there. You can then approach your plan as if it were a formal project. There is a saying that's used a lot in project management circles that may help you, "Plan your work, then work your plan."

Having taught project management for several years the most popular approach was to plan everything in detail from start to finish. If you

STEP 6: PLAN YOUR WAY FORWARD

knew exactly what you wanted to achieve then this seemed a logical way to go about things. However, this structured way of managing projects didn't always work out well in every case. Some projects were clear about the direction they were currently heading in but uncertain as to their final destination. So someone came up with an alternative way of managing these adaptable projects and called it the "Agile" method. This allowed you to take a good guess at where you would end up but only encouraged you to plan the next step in detail. Once you'd completed the first step you'd look again at the long-term goal and then adjust course and plan the second step in detail. You would keep moving forward step by step until you finally reached a point where you could say the project was complete.

Could an Agile approach work better for you when thinking about the future? If you're not sure exactly where you want to end up, do you still have a general sense of direction? If so, is there a logical next step that you can take? Could you put off deciding which direction your second step will go in until after you complete the first step? If you're heading into new territory it's quite likely you'll discover new things while taking your first step. What you learn will then help you when it comes to deciding what your second step should be.

When planning to move forward, don't panic. It's better to set yourself a goal for the next three to six months and work towards it than to stay paralysed by fear because you can't map out the whole of your life. Sometimes discovering your life purpose can feel a bit like driving through fog. You might need to take things slowly for a while and concentrate harder. The fog may lift at times and you can start seeing further ahead – until it closes in again. Don't worry, proceed with caution, keep going and eventually you will come out the other side.

If it helps you, develop short, medium and long-term goals. If your vision could take 25 years to achieve I'd encourage you to develop a plan that sets goals for where you expect to be in 10 years time, plus also five years, three years, one year and six months from now. What you need is a set of clear steps that lead you one by one to achieve your overall goal. If the distance between any of the steps seems too great to stride across then you need to insert an additional step.

If what you're looking to do is completely new or uncertain, I'd recommend pilot-testing your idea small scale before committing yourself big time. This will give you the opportunity to make sure your idea is viable and surface any previously unforeseen problems. Through pilot-testing you will also acquire a wealth of knowledge and useful contacts. By proving what you are trying to do works you can also build confidence in other people who may want to get involved or whose support you need. You can also reassure yourself and help to overcome any doubts you may have had but were afraid to tell others about.

On the subject of planning, some would suggest it's wise to have a "Plan B". There are two ways of looking at this: First, common sense says that things don't always work out as planned and it's useful to have a fall-back position. Second, if you give yourself an escape route you will be more tempted to take it. It partly depends upon you and your level of motivation. It's also affected by the size and nature of the vision that you're working towards. If you are risk-averse, preferring to play it safe, then having a Plan B will give you more confidence in going for Plan A. That's because you can see that if things don't work out you already have a contingency plan in place and are ready to change course if needed. My advice though is if you create a Plan B, file it away somewhere safe and leave it there. Only look at it if you really need to otherwise you could get distracted and give up on your Plan A.

If you're prepared to risk all and prefer a "do or die" approach you may decide it's better to push yourself into a position where you just have to make it work. When ancient Greek warriors landed in an area they wished to conquer, their first task was to set fire to their own boats. Having destroyed their means of escape they were forced to fight for their lives and conquer the land. Many entrepreneurs testify that by jumping in at the deep end and refusing to think about a Plan B they found a way to realize their dream. Many admit it's a high-risk strategy and they had to work very hard to achieve their goal, but they still made it. If this approach resonates with you, go for it!

○○○○○○○○○○○○○○○○○○○○○○○○○○○○○○○○○○○○○○○

EXERCISE: Plan your way forward
Get clear about what you want to do. Craft your Plan A. Start with the end in mind and work backwards or take an Agile approach and just plan your next step. Decide if you want a Plan B or not. If you do, sketch it out. Give yourself short, medium and long-term goals to aim for. Write your plan out; don't just keep it in your head. Remember the saying, "Plan your work then work your plan."

○○○○○○○○○○○○○○○○○○○○○○○○○○○○○○○○○○○○○○○

Re-align your life

If you've worked through the previous steps and discovered you are already close to living out your true purpose, great! You might only need to change a few things to achieve your goals. However, if you now realize you are off-track and need to change direction be reassured, you've already laid the foundation on which to build your new future. With a clear mission and personal vision in place you know where you want to get to and why. You can also lean heavily on your values and conscience to guide you. For energy look to your core motivator and remember how what you are doing is worthwhile. Either use the strengths you have or develop new ones you need so you can do what you want to do.

Where you feel you may want to re-align your life look at where you want to be, where you are now, then think about how to bridge the gap. It may be you need to give up some of the things you are currently doing before you have the time and space to take on something new. One of the hardest decisions you may face is in trying to choose between what is good and what is best. Good things are perfectly okay in themselves but they might not align fully with your newly defined goal. Good things can help others and yourself but may still deflect you from your true purpose. If so, you may need to say "No" to the good to free you up to say "Yes" to the best.

If your intended change in direction is going to affect those who are close to you then think carefully about it. In the next chapter we'll talk a bit about working through the challenges of talking to close friends and family. If it involves setting up a new business venture or major changes to your personal finances then I'd again suggest talking to a financial advisor.

To help you work out what needs changing in your life try asking the following questions:

- *Is everything I do a reflection of my main mission in life?*
- *Is anything I do deflecting me away from my desired vision?*
- *Is there something I'm doing that conflicts with my core values?*
- *Do I feel uneasy in my conscience about anything?*
- *Am I lacking skills or knowledge that I need to achieve my objectives?*
- *What is it I need to give up or reduce to help me get back on track?*

Having identified what needs changing think through how you can make that change happen. It might be saying "No" to repeated requests for you to take on extra responsibilities at work. You may decide to set aside one of your hobbies to go back to college to develop new skills. Or you could decide now is the time to step down from one of your social responsibilities to free up time to start working on your new project. Whatever it is you've identified, make a note of it and ideally put it on your to-do list and plan when you're going to do something about it.

STEP 6: PLAN YOUR WAY FORWARD

Take a step today

Even with a clear plan of where you want to be and a list of things you would like to change in life, there is still a need to take action. I've met people with a clear vision, a sound business plan, a recognition of what needs to change for them to live their dream and yet they still fail to make it happen. Carol was one such person. Desiring to change her life, she planned to start a small-scale catering business working from home. She'd researched the market, the competition, her potential customers and created a sound business plan. There was every indication that it should work. Then she stopped herself from going any further; she failed to take the next step.

There's an old Chinese saying: "A journey of a thousand miles starts with a single step." The only way to reach your goal is to take a step in the right direction. Carol had done her homework and could see the next step but failed to take it. Perhaps if she had broken down that first big step into a series of smaller steps she may have ventured out and got her business underway after all. So my advice to you is to identify a simple step that you can take today that will help you move forwards in some way. What is it you can do today that will get you moving towards your freshly clarified purpose in life? It might be making just one phone call, or researching on the internet, or visiting a friend to talk things over. Whatever it is, plan to do something today to get yourself moving. Each time you do something you will feel better knowing that you've moved a little closer to your goal.

Here are some more suggestions that can help you in taking your first steps towards your new venture. Try to keep things simple, achievable and ideally visible so you've can see the a result for your efforts:

- Create a dedicated workspace where you can sit down and work at your idea

- De-clutter your computer and set up some new folders just for your new venture

- Enrol on that business start-up course you've been thinking about lately
- Make that vision board and hang it on the wall where you can see it
- Buy yourself a good notebook you can carry around with you in which you can jot down your ideas as they come to you – and write something in it!
- Set aside 30 minutes each day in your diary for your new project. (This adds up to two working days every month. Just imagine what you can achieve in two full days.)

If it helps, promise yourself a small reward for achieving your first step, something that makes you feel good inside. Again, don't be put off if you can't see the whole picture yet, keep moving forwards. Trust in the advice of Martin Luther King Jr: "Take the first step in faith. You don't have to see the whole staircase. Just take the first step."

Key thoughts to take away:

This step has focused on bringing things together from the previous steps and helped you plan for your future. Key thoughts to take away include:

- Taking responsibility and being proactive will make you effective
- Working out what you don't want helps you see what you do want
- Asking yourself empowering questions leads to success
- Knowing your priorities keeps you focused

STEP 6: PLAN YOUR WAY FORWARD

- Your mission reminds you why you're here; your vision where you're heading
- Thinking SMART sharpens your focus
- Thinking practically is part of thinking purposefully
- Starting with the end in mind helps you plan your path
- Taking a step today is the way to make your dream come true

With a clear plan in place (even if it's just for the next step), you are now ready to move forwards. To make sure you succeed there are a number of things you can do. The next chapter will give you plenty of hints and tips to help you prepare for success.

o o o

STEP 7:
PREPARE FOR SUCCESS

NAVIGATE CHANGE AND OVERCOME OBSTACLES

○ ○ ○

STEP 7
Prepare For Success
Navigate Change and Overcome Obstacles

o o o

*"That some achieve great success,
is proof to all that others can achieve it as well."*
(Abraham Lincoln – former president of the United States)

o o o

Prepare yourself...

ZARA'S CHILDREN HAD SETTLED WELL in school and for the first time in years she had time on her hands. Initially she filled it by catching up with friends and socializing. After a while she felt a stirring inside, feeling that she wanted to do something more with her life. She had a growing interest in photography and so bought herself a nice camera. She enjoyed taking shots of happy moments her family shared on film. Others recognized her natural gifting and commented on her photos. She was even asked by a friend to take the photos at their wedding. Zara realized that this could become something bigger than just a hobby so she enrolled on a two-year photography course. After that she took a further course in preparing to start your own business. Zara then found a small studio and launched out on her own. But to her it's more than just taking nice photos; Zara works hard to portray happiness in pictures so others can enjoy precious moments forever. When it comes to wedding photography, she unobtrusively stays close to the bride and manages to catch those brief glances, the hilarious laughter and the deep emotion that so many other photographers miss.

STEP 7: PREPARE FOR SUCCESS

Zara had a dream that grew with time. To make that dream a reality she hatched a plan. Taking one step at a time she developed her skills and took action to launch her business. At each step, as well as taking practical action she was preparing herself mentally. The psychological side of preparing yourself is probably even more important than the physical dimension. Making life-changing decisions and taking action can affect you as a person. Bear in mind that all personal growth takes place outside your comfort zone. There may be times when you feel unsettled, disorientated and challenged. Knowing this can happen and being ready for it will help you cope better. That's what this chapter is going to equip you to do. You'll read more about how Zara navigated such challenges a little later.

Appreciate how far you've come already

Whether you realize it or not, you've already made a lot of progress. For a start, you took action in picking up and reading this book. Working through the exercises will have put you in touch with yourself in a much deeper way. New insights you've gained have equipped and empowered you to look at life differently. You now have a clearer perspective on life. You also recognize what's most worthwhile to invest your time and energies into. You've thought through what you are good at and what you want to do with the rest of your life. From the last chapter you would have created a plan to help you get to where you want to be.

Most people never make the effort you've made to think seriously about life and what they're going to do with it. Be encouraged, you are now in the top few per cent of people on this planet. Just for a moment, with an attitude of humility, compliment yourself on the progress you have made. Try saying aloud, "[your name], well done! You've invested time and effort into discovering your unique purpose in life. As a result you can now live a more fulfilling and satisfying life. You will also have the greatest impact for good on those around you. Congratulations!"

Prepare for change

With a clear vision and a workable plan in place, it's time to prepare for change. As we've said before, it's generally better to be proactive and plan for it than be reactive and have it forced upon you. However, even if you've been pushed into change through no choice of your own, such as being made redundant, you can still choose how you will respond to it. There is a saying that as one door closes another always opens. This may be true but sometimes it feels as if there's a long hallway between the two doors. But take heart, the new door might be just around the corner and only barely out of sight.

When it comes to planning a change in life there are often two options open to you. You can take drastic action and change everything or you can move slowly forward changing one thing at a time. Choosing a sudden and significant change can assist you in making the most progress towards your goal in the shortest time, but it can be quite disruptive to life. Taking an incremental approach is often safer but will mean you might need to give yourself more time to get to where you want to be. Again, the choice is yours and depends on your personal circumstances, commitments, the project you have in mind and your appetite for risk.

Like Zara, part of your preparation for change may be to develop your knowledge and skills to ensure you are ready to take on the challenges of the future. Knowing what you want to do and where you want to go provides a sense of direction that guides you. For a few though, there's another way forward that's worth considering. I've heard it referred to as "the creative pause". Some people are unable to see a new way forward because of the busyness and distractions of life and what they're already committed to. If that's you then perhaps it would pay you to take a creative pause. To do so you need to put aside some of the things which aren't essential in life right at this moment and free up time to give yourself space to think. In a more radical approach,

STEP 7: PREPARE FOR SUCCESS

I've known people who have given up jobs, taken time out at a retreat centre or gone on a long holiday to give themselves the opportunity to reflect on life and where they go from here. For some there also seems to be an incubation period where their dream needs to grow within them before it can finally be brought to birth. If you have conceived a dream but are still in the early stages of your pregnancy, enjoy this time. Allow yourself to grow with your dream and make the necessary preparations before your expected due date. The time will come soon enough if you keep working towards it.

On the subject of creative pauses and incubation periods it could be worth mentioning a book written by William Bridges called *Managing Transitions*. In it he talks about a neutral zone that people pass through between letting go of the past and taking hold of the future. To illustrate this he discusses the example of the Jewish nation after they had fled for their lives out of Egypt. Bridges points out that they didn't walk straight into the promised land. Instead, they spent time wandering in the wilderness. This in between phase taught them many things that proved useful for their future, even though it felt disorientating and confusing at the time. In a similar way, don't be surprised if you feel disorientated if you've let go of the past and haven't arrived at your new future yet. Realize this is natural. Many of the Jews felt a desire to return to the stability and predictability of their previous life in Egypt. You too may be tempted to give into the tug that pulls you backwards to what you'd previously been doing. At that point you may need to reflect on your mission, vision and values and find a way to encourage yourself to keep going.

Count the cost

We've already discussed the practicality of counting the financial cost to pursuing your dream. Many years ago, I visited a family and talked with them briefly on this issue of counting the cost when it comes to pursuing a purposeful pathway. A little while later they gave up everything and took up a missionary role to help those worse off than themselves in a poor and developing country. They knew it was the right thing for them to do. What I didn't find out until many years later was that they had sold their share of the family business and gave the proceeds away before heading for distant shores. While this surprised me, what really stopped me in my tracks was discovering that their share of the business was worth more than 50 million dollars. They truly counted the cost, paid the price, then pursued their purpose.

It's worth mentioning that there may also be emotional costs. Pursuing a new venture can be both energising and tiring at the same time. Remember Bob and Mary who changed their lives to follow their dream of living a more self-sufficient lifestyle? As well as the physical tiredness of cultivating and harvesting their own food, the pressure of living in a caravan with two young children for three years while they worked at building their house certainly proved challenging at times. Then there's the issue of possible changes to relationships. Family and friends can sometimes find it a struggle when you decide you're going to head off in a new direction in life. Within the television series, *Wanted Down Under*, families are given the chance to spend a week visiting Australia or New Zealand to see if they would like to relocate there. After looking at jobs, houses, schools and other facets of a possible new life they could have, they are shown a video of friends and family from back home. I don't remember one episode where there were no tears as parents, grandparents, siblings and others talked about how difficult they found it to come to terms with their loved ones moving so far away.

If you're thinking of a major change that could impact your relationships with your friends and family then try to anticipate how they may react. No doubt you may be excited about your future and what you're hoping to achieve but try to see it from their perspective. How will your plans affect them? How less often might they see you? How will your commitment to your cause change your focus of attention

STEP 7: PREPARE FOR SUCCESS

and the way you relate to them? That's not to say you shouldn't chase after your dream, I'm just trying to make you aware that there may be an emotional cost to outworking your plan.

Let go of the past

We talked previously about living in the past, present or future. While we live in the present and can dream about the future there are times when the past can hold us back. One way this happens is when we've enjoyed successes or good times with a particular group of people. We can long for "the good old days" that were filled with fun and a sense of achievement. The danger is we can become overly nostalgic and spend too much time looking in our rear view mirror. In doing so we can take our eyes off the road ahead and miss out on an even more exciting and rewarding journey. There are times when we need to acknowledge all that was good about the past but yet make a resolute decision to focus on the future and move forward. You cannot take hold of the future if you are forever hanging on to the past.

Then there are some who are troubled by past mistakes and failures. If you've tried and failed previously then I can understand it if you are hesitant to try again. However, past mistakes and failures should not hold us back. There's no point trying to deny what has happened but realize that today is a new day. You are free to make a fresh start from this day onwards. Ignore those who remind you of past failures. Rise above the noise of their distracting chatter. Accept the past, learn from it and move on. Only you can choose whether you will let yourself be bound by the past or set free to enjoy the future. No-one else has the right to make that decision for you.

Remember the ancient Greek warriors we mentioned previously? They not only let go of the past, by burning their boats they firmly shut the door on it. Many religions use some form of ritual whereby new followers symbolically show they have turned from their past way of life and are committing to a new direction. This includes making vows, wearing special clothing or being baptized. Such outward actions both serves as a message to others and reminder to themselves of their personal commitment to their new cause. Is there something you can do that in some way illustrates your break with the past?

Clear out your clutter

Part of letting go of the past may involve you in resolving unfinished business and clearing out your clutter. Clutter can be physical and psychological. Clutter can distract and drain you. People who I've met who have had a good clear out usually get all excited and tell me how much better they feel once they've got rid of stuff they no longer need or want. I remember the last time we moved house. The charity shops and recycle centre benefitted from yet more donations. If you've been hoarding things just in case they might come in handy one day, ask yourself whether you really need to keep it all or not. I've come to realize it's always a good time to have a spring-clean – even if it's in the middle of winter.

As well as freeing up physical space, you may benefit from liberating some psychological space. Are there any loose ends that would benefit from being tied up? If you've not done so already I'd suggest writing or updating your will. Are there unresolved tensions in any relationships you have? Is there a way to make the peace? Are you committed to a cause or charity that you feel tied to but want to break free from? Is now the time to make the break? Just like you can't take hold of the future until you've let go of the past, sometimes you won't have the space available to receive something new into your life until you've first removed some clutter from the past.

It may pay you to review your current commitments and social engagements. Do these support and compliment your newly clarified goals in life? If so, great! If not, are there some that you should give up?

STEP 7: PREPARE FOR SUCCESS

As we've already said, it helps to recognize that you are not indispensible. Stepping down from a role can give others an opportunity to rise to the occasion. Indeed, there may even be someone who has secretly been longing to take over from you. Even if there isn't, is it right to stay shackled to something you know deep down is holding you back?

Free up your time

Would you like an extra day each week to do all the other things you'd like to do? How about just one additional hour each evening? You're not on your own. Time seems to be in short supply. When you are young you feel you have all the time in the world and it seems as if time drags slowly by. As you age you can start to think that someone has speeded up the conveyor belt as the years start flying past you. The more you want to do the less time there seems to be.

The truth is that we are all given the same number of minutes each day and they are all consumed at the same rate. It's not how much time you have but what you do with it that counts. Many years ago I used to teach Time Management as a subject. In reality though, there is no way you can manage time. You cannot stop or turn back the clock. It marches on relentlessly. The only thing you can do is learn to manage yourself within the context of time. The secret is to invest yourself in those things that matter most to you – even if other things never get done. Good managers learn to delegate. They pass on to others those tasks that would not be the best use of their time. In doing so they free up time for more important and valuable tasks.

Let's suppose you want to set up a new organization to improve the quality of drinking water for people in developing countries. Do you think you need to create the website, develop the marketing brochures, write all the letters and clean the offices yourself? No, of course not. You would do better to invest your time in meeting key people and drafting the key messages you want to communicate while you ask others to do the technical and fine detail work. One question that challenged me some years ago was, "What is it you can do that only you can do?" This is the thing you should be investing most of your time into. Again I'd remind you to find your key priorities and then build your life around them.

Remember what Stephen Covey said in his book *First Things First*? Live your life by the compass not the clock. Focus on aligning what you do with your vision and values first. After that you can work out what appointments and commitments you want to fit into your day. Once you know what's most important to you then it's much easier to answer the question, "Is what I'm doing right now the best use of my time?" If it's not then find a way to delegate it to someone else or just stop doing it. Life is too short to waste your time doing things that add little value.

○○○○○○○○○○○○○○○○○○○○○○○○○○○○○○○○○○○

EXERCISE: Freeing up time

When you reach the point where you know you need to free up more time ask yourself, "Is this the best use of my time?" Try asking the question repeatedly for a whole week. Ask it regularly (try every hour), ask it randomly (at any time of the day without warning), and ask it reluctantly (when you already know the answer is going to be "No"). Identify those things that should be minimized or managed out of your life. This will free up time you can then give to higher value activities.

○○○○○○○○○○○○○○○○○○○○○○○○○○○○○○○○○○○

Think positive

One thing W Clement Stone and his friend Napoleon Hill were known for was their positive mental attitude. They actually wrote a book called *Success through a Positive Mental Attitude*. In it they gave many accounts of people who had achieved success as a direct result of a conscious choice to cultivate and maintain a positive mental attitude.

STEP 7: PREPARE FOR SUCCESS

As an example of the power of negative thought, you may have heard of a railroad worker named Nick who accidentally locked himself in a boxcar overnight. Realising it was a refrigerated unit he feared he would freeze to death. He wrote a note inside the boxcar saying how cold he felt adding, "...these will probably be my last words". They were. The next morning fellow workers found him dead. The doctor that examined him said he showed all the classic signs of hypothermia. What Nick didn't know was that the unit wasn't working and the temperature was well above freezing. Nick didn't die due to the cold, he died by the power of his own thoughts.

Another example of the power of thought is found in the story of Russian weightlifter Vasily Alexeyev. In the 1970s it was thought impossible to lift 500 pounds overhead. Vasily held the world record and had previously lifted 499.9 pounds. Then in one important competition his trainers gave him a set of weights telling him it was a repeat of his previous record of 499.9 pounds. After he succeeded with the lift they confessed they had lied. Vasily had just lifted 500.5 pounds. With the 500 pound barrier broken and confidence renewed, Vasily went on to eventually lift more than 560 pounds.

Your thoughts control your beliefs and in turn these determine your actions. Your actions are the things that lead to results – but they ultimately come from your thoughts. Your thoughts are powerful. You can set limits or break them by the power of thought. Beware of any self-criticism, negative thoughts or words. Eradicate them and replace them with positives. One phrase that has become popular in today's world is "No problem". The trouble with this phrase is that when you ask someone for something you don't want to hear them say "No" to you. Neither do you want to hear about problems, what you want is solutions. Try responding to other's requests with a more positive phrase such as "I'd be happy to". This way you're telling yourself you are going to be more happy. You might think I'm being too pernickety but try it for a while and see what difference it makes.

○○○○○○○○○○○○○○○○○○○○○○○○○○○○○○○○○○○○○○

EXERCISE: Go on a negativity fast

Now you can see some of the benefit from cultivating a positive mental attitude I offer you a new challenge. Go on a negativity fast. What I mean by that is to cut out from your daily life any negative thinking, speaking or actions. Do this for at least one whole week but ideally try it for a month. You never know, this could be a new and helpful habit you may want to keep for your lifetime.

○○○○○○○○○○○○○○○○○○○○○○○○○○○○○○○○○○○○○○

Feed your soul

Have you come across the *Chicken Soup for the Soul* series of books? Jack Canfield and Mark Victor Hansen have spent years collecting more than 100,000 personal stories about life, love and people. Their aim is to bring hope and inspiration to others. Some of the stories are funny, a few are deeply moving, but they're all aimed at providing encouragement in some shape or form. Reading such books can give you a lift and spur you on in your own efforts to live life to the full and pursue your own purpose.

As well as reading books you could listen to instructional or motivational audio recordings that can help you stay focused on your goals. If you do much driving then listening to such recordings can be a good way to make best use of your driving time. Online videos are another source of encouragement worth considering. Whatever media you use, listening to and being inspired by others is one way to help you stay on track. We all need encouragement from time to time.

If you can, find ways to meet up with others who share your desire to do something worthwhile or are passionate about a cause. Your shared enthusiasm and common interests will help to nourish your soul. Places to find like-minded people include clubs, meet-up groups and mastermind groups. Having led mastermind groups in the past I've seen

STEP 7: PREPARE FOR SUCCESS

people come in feeling a little empty and after a couple of hours of mutual encouragement, they've left with renewed vitality.

Another way to feed your soul is by using positive affirmations. As well as your thoughts having the power to change your future, so do your words. Whatever your mouth says your ears hear and your mind starts to believe. By changing the words you use you can influence the thoughts you think and the results you achieve. Positive affirmations built around your vision and objectives can keep you focused and help you work towards their achievement. Once you've written out your affirmation carry it with you, repeating it several times each day until you can say it easily from memory. The more you say it the more your mind will come to believe it.

○ ○

EXERCISE: Write and use a positive affirmation
Try creating a positive affirmation you can repeat several times each day. Here's an example you could adapt: "Every day I am moving closer to my goal of [state your goal] by using my strengths of [state your strengths], knowing that what I'm doing is worthwhile and beneficial for others."

○ ○

Overcome obstacles

Obstacles come in different shapes and sizes. Some are blatant and hit you head-on; others are subtle and seem to creep up on you from behind. Remember Zara the photographer? One practical obstacle that initially held her back was the lack of business knowledge – so she took a course and learnt how to set up her own business. After a little while she became aware of another challenge. She had previously enjoyed a relaxed social life where she met with other women to pass the time of day in their favorite coffee shops. As Zara invested more time in her business a tension surfaced. Her friends didn't understand her drive to do something new with her life and Zara felt as if they were trying to pull her back towards her previous way of life. Maybe one or two felt a little envy, jealousy or personal challenge as Zara was now doing something they lacked the courage to do. Zara made the hard decision to put her passion first, even if it meant less time socializing with her original friends. Then unexpectedly she started to meet new people, including other women who were starting out in business. Many of these understood her desire to do something new and shared a similar passion. Zara is now building a new network of supportive friends.

Don't be surprised if some of your current friends and family don't understand what you are doing or why. Sadly, some become jealous, envious that you are changing your life when they would love to but choose not to for whatever reason. Some may resent you moving forward in a new direction as they feel you are rejecting them personally. Those that are dependent on you (financially or otherwise) may be afraid they will lose your support if you take off in a new direction. For a few, your future journey is so far outside their way of seeing life they will never understand what you are trying to do. Don't take it personally; it's their problem, not yours. They have to come to terms with what's happening and will hopefully take a more mature attitude towards you in time.

As we've said, obstacles come in different shapes and sizes. What you need is a little wisdom in looking at them and asking if you should climb over them, push them out of the way, go around them or just occasionally, take a detour and head off in a new direction. By asking yourself the empowering question of "How can I deal with this obstacle?" your subconscious is likely to help you find which is the most appropriate way forward. If you're really at a loss as to how best to approach it then finding someone to talk to about it may help. Usually, by maintaining a firm focus on your mission and vision, you should be able to find your way through to overcome any obstacle that presents you with a

STEP 7: PREPARE FOR SUCCESS

challenge. Three obstacles that people regularly face when setting out to pursue their purpose are fear, rejection and failure. Therefore, we'll spend a bit of time looking at each of these.

Face your fears

Very often the biggest barrier that holds people back is fear. Fear has been defined as "Fantasized Evidence Appearing Real". Common fears that people experience when they look forward to creating a different future include fear of the unknown, fear of failure, fear of what others will think.

In her best-selling book, *Feel the Fear and Do It Anyway*, Susan Jeffers tackles fear head on. She points out that the root of fear is an underlying belief that we can't handle whatever it is we fear. Because people fear failure many never attempt to do new things in the first place. Those who fear rejection by friends and family can also hold back from doing something that could affect their current relationships.

The antidote to fear, according to Jeffers, is to "develop more trust in your ability to handle whatever comes your way". It sounds too simple yet her book unfolds this truth with numerous case studies of people she has helped over the past 25 years. By asking yourself "What's the worst that can happen?" and then working out how you would cope if it were to happen, you immediately weaken the grip that fear has had on you. Another tactic is to focus on the benefits of pushing through the fear and achieving your desired goal. This should help to motivate and encourage you.

Feeling fear is normal. Just about everyone feels fear when they face new situations and challenges. This includes sporting heroes, successful businesspeople and courageous politicians. The thing that will make a difference for you is your willingness to confront the fear and your decision to push forward despite the fear. Courage is not the absence of fear; it's persevering in the face of fear. That's why Jeffer's book title conveys such a powerful message, *Feel the Fear and Do It Anyway!* She points out that, "The only way to get rid of the fear of doing something is to go out and do it."

I've applied this to my own life several times over. I've suffered from a fear of heights so I pushed myself to paint the outside of our house climbing nearly 30 feet up a ladder. I've also had a fear of flying, so I volunteered for a teaching assignment where I knew beforehand I would have to take ten flights over a period of several months. Sure, the intensity of the fear reaches a crescendo as you start doing the thing you fear, but the relief and excitement you experience from actually having pushed though it is far greater. Oddly enough, in some ways I was disappointed both when I'd finished painting the house and when I stepped off the plane for the last time because I knew the opportunity to face and overcome my fears had been taken away from me.

Now please, even though I may sound like I'm encouraging you to go out and tackle your fears head on, I'd also advise you not to take unnecessary risks and put yourself in harm's way. We need to use some common sense here. I wouldn't suggest you should go swimming in the muddy rivers of Africa to overcome a fear of crocodiles. What I'd advise you to do is stop, turn around, then analyse your fear. Ask yourself, "What exactly am I afraid of? What are the negative consequences I am expecting? Why have I felt I couldn't handle this? How can I develop my trust and confidence to the level that I am able to handle it?"

ooooooooooooooooooooooooooooooooooooooooo

EXERCISE: Overcome your fears

Choose a fear that has affected your life in some way. Analyse it. Get a clear understanding of how it has held you back and what you're missing out on. Identify the benefits you gain from overcoming it. Work out how you would handle the situation you fear if it were to happen. If you need to, get some support in place before you tackle your fear. Now take action in some way towards overcoming your fear. For example, if you're afraid of flying read

STEP 7: PREPARE FOR SUCCESS

about planes and how they are made. Talk to people that have flown recently. Think about how confident pilots must be to do the job they do. Visit an airport and watch the planes taking off and landing. Book yourself on a short pleasure flight or an internal connection flight. Maybe you'll end up buying yourself an around the world ticket!

○ ○

Reject rejection

Just now I mentioned *Chicken Soup for the Soul*. Did you know that Jack Canfield and Mark Victor Hansen were rejected over 130 times in their search for a publisher before someone eventually said "Yes" to their idea? No doubt they took on board the attitude of a fellow American businessman, Bo Bennett, who declared, "Rejection is nothing more than a necessary step in the pursuit of success." Too many people give up when they meet rejection. You could be tempted to also. What would have happened if Jack and Mark had given up after the first rejection, or the twenty-first, or the hundred and twenty-first? The books would not have been published, they would not have become wealthy, but more than that, millions of people would have missed out on the encouraging and inspirational stories they captured and shared. The world would have been a poorer place.

Many years ago there was a hard-working man whose business failed. After being given a Social Security payment he looked at it and said, "My life isn't over and I'm not going to sit in a rocking chair and take money from the government." Then aged 65, he went out and tried to get other people to pay him for an idea he had for a recipe. It's said he was turned away 1,009 times over a period of two years before someone saw the potential and decided to give it a try. Now fifty years later this one recipe has multiplied into the world's largest restaurant chain with over 37,000 Kentucky Fried Chicken outlets in over 110 countries. Colonel Harland Sanders just chose to reject rejection.

Here's a short resume of someone who repeatedly experienced failure and rejection:

- Aged 21 – failed in business
- Aged 22 – defeated in a legislative race
- Aged 24 – failed in business again
- Aged 27 – had a nervous breakdown
- Aged 34 – lost a congressional race
- Aged 39 – failed to be re-elected to congress
- Aged 45 – lost a senatorial race
- Aged 47 – failed in an effort to become vice-president
- Aged 49 – failed another senatorial race

Do you recognize who this is? With a track record like that, if you were their friend, might you have suggested that after thirty years of trying to get somewhere in politics it was time to give up? But this man didn't and at age 52 Abraham Lincoln became the 16th President of the United States.

If you are tempted to fall into a pit of despair after being rejected, don't! Remember these examples of people who went on to succeed and encourage yourself to reject rejection. Try approaching rejection in the way that Sylvester Stallone does. He said, "I take rejection as someone blowing a bugle in my ear to wake me up and get going, rather than retreat."

Make failure your friend

"What? I thought you were talking about success. Now you're telling me to embrace failure. That sounds crazy!" Just like I said courage

STEP 7: PREPARE FOR SUCCESS

is not the absence of fear but persevering in the face of fear, success isn't the absence of failure but persevering in the face of failure. We all experience failure in some way when things don't work out like we'd planned. We have expectations and when things don't turn out like we'd expected we think something must have gone wrong. Often, the truth is that there were other factors involved that had an impact on the result that we hadn't anticipated or couldn't foresee when we first set out. Life happens, things change, we don't spot something – and we end up with a different result compared to what we had hoped for.

Just because you experience a failure doesn't mean you are a failure. Don't take it so personally. If things happened which were outside your control detach yourself from it emotionally. See it as a cause and effect situation. If you failed to foresee something also don't be too harsh on yourself. Treat it as a learning experience and use it to empower you to make more insightful and informed decisions about any future action you may take. Apparently Thomas Edison failed repeatedly when he was trying to create the electric light bulb. So some say, when he was confronted over his supposed failure he replied, "I have not failed. I've just found 10,000 ways that won't work." He didn't give up and now we all benefit from his perseverance. And what word of caution and encouragement does he offer us in view of the repeated failures he experienced? "Our greatest weakness lies in giving up. The most certain way to succeed is always to try just one more time."

A healthy way to learn from failure is to treat it as a case study. Step outside the situation for a moment. Ask yourself what happened and why. Treat it as if it's a scientific experiment and not a court case. What you're looking for is understanding that leads to new knowledge. Avoid trying to pin the blame on anyone else so you can walk away from it saying, "It wasn't my fault things went wrong." In fact, once you've got a grasp on the situation it's helpful to step back into the situation and to take personal responsibility. Admit where you may have messed up. Assure yourself that you will do better next time. Get up, dust yourself off and try again.

In his book *Your Roadmap for Success*, John Maxwell says, "Unsuccessful people are often so afraid of failure and rejection that they spend their whole lives avoiding risks or decisions that could lead to failure. They don't realize that success is based on their ability to fail and continue trying." Now are you starting to see why I'm encouraging you to view failure as your friend? Failure is another one of your teachers who can help you learn what doesn't work, how things happen, and how you can find new ways forward that can prove to be more effective. The more you fail the more you can learn and the more effective you can become. As long as you have an open mind you can learn from what happens and move closer to success. I'd suggest you can only really fail when you fail to learn from the situation.

Just in case you may still be asking yourself, "What if it doesn't work out?" consider this. Even if things don't work out the way you've planned, it's probably better that you tried, failed, then learnt something, rather than you never tried and lived the rest of your life with regret. Do you really want to live out your years wondering what life would have been like had you made the effort to pursue your dream? And there's another question I could ask you, "What if it does work out?" Try taking your eyes off what could go wrong and focus for a minute on what could go right. Surely, it's got to be worth a try hasn't it?

Build your support team

One of the best ways to stay motivated when times get tough is to have a supportive network of people you can fall back on. These can be family, friends, work colleagues or others. Having been part of two mastermind groups I've learnt the value of investing time with like-minded individuals who share a common pathway in life. Knowing there are others who also want to see you succeed is a great encouragement.

As you change you may find that others struggle to relate to the new you. In time though, some of your previously negative or doubting

STEP 7: PREPARE FOR SUCCESS

friends will be attracted to the way of life you have chosen. They too may wish to walk alongside you on your journey. They may even ask you how you managed to lift yourself out of the place from which you have come. You then become their coach and mentor as you pass on what you have learned.

If you're looking for support or someone to bounce your ideas off of, try to find people who are open-minded. One of the problems you can encounter with many career coaches is that they look at what you've done so far in life and then assume you will want a similar job, but with a different employer. They limit your future by confining you within the previous boundaries that you've worked within. Herminia Ibarra wrote a thought-provoking article for the Harvard Business Review titled, *How to Stay Stuck in the Wrong Career*. In it she said, "Finding a new job always requires networking outside our usual circles. We get ideas and job leads by branching out." She referred to this as "shifting connections" explaining that this is "the practice of finding people who can help us see and grow into our new selves". She concludes, "To make a break with the past, we must venture into unknown networks – and not just for job leads. Often it is strangers who are best equipped to help us see who we are becoming."

But how can you create a supportive network around you? Try to find people who can fulfil the following:

- They have time to listen

- They are looking out for your interests, not just their own

- They can relate to the ideas you want to discuss

- They are positive, optimistic and encouraging

One way of keeping yourself on track is to make yourself accountable to someone else. Asking someone to check up on you at regular intervals can help keep you focused. Knowing that you will be asked, "What have you done in this past month?" can have a sobering effect. This is why some people employ a coach – not to tell them what to do but to ask them what they've done. You could enlist the help of a spouse, partner, friend, family member or work colleague. Whoever it is, choose someone who won't let you get away with giving them a wishy-washy answer. They don't need to come down hard on you but they should challenge you if you haven't achieved your goals and ask you, "Why not?" Who could you make yourself accountable to?

Get on board with a coach

Consider hiring a coach if you're looking for some specialized help. A good life coach can help you clarify your goals and achieve them, supporting you to overcome obstacles and break through blockages. When looking for a coach find one who shares the same personal values and understands what you are trying to achieve. When I previously hired a coach, I sought out someone who had already achieved what I wanted to do and got to where I wanted to be. If you're stuck in a hole there's no point asking for help from someone who's also stuck in the hole with you. Instead, find someone who has climbed out of the hole and ask them how they did it. Maybe they took years to figure out how to get out of the hole. If that's the case you can benefit from all their hard work and take a short-cut as you learn from them. You could save yourself years of effort and wasted money by getting help from the right coach.

I've been in meetings where millionaire business-people have openly said that one of the things that made the biggest difference to their success was when they hired a coach. Sometimes they did it to learn a specific skill, other times it was to help them develop their mindset. When you hire a coach you're investing in your future. Working one-to-one with an experienced coach is probably the fastest way for you to make progress. Following that, becoming a member of a coaching, mentoring or mastermind group can also be a great way to learn and develop.

STEP 7: PREPARE FOR SUCCESS

A quick word about partners, spouses and families

Hopefully your family will be completely supportive of you and your efforts. Start with the belief that your family would want the best for you. It's great when they can share in your joy. Ultimately, if you're living a more fulfilling life then you'll be more at peace with yourself and have more to give to those around you. Because they love you, they should be your greatest supporters.

If you're thinking about making a major change in life, try to choose the right moment to talk it over with your family. Bear in mind that while you may have been thinking things through for a while, what you say may be new to them. They may need time to come to terms with what you've been considering. If they appear hesitant or unclear, try to be patient and ask them what it is that they're finding difficult.

If you have children, it's wise to talk things through with your partner before saying too much to your children – especially if they are young. Even though they can cope with an enormous amount of change, children like stability and certainty. If you suddenly announce you are going to sell up and head off to the Amazon jungle to save the rain forest don't be surprised if they protest. Think about things from their perspective. Will they have to give up their friends? What about their schooling? And if you were their age how might you feel about giving up a warm, dry bedroom for an earth-covered floor in a mud-hut?

If your children are in their late teens be prepared for the possibility that they may not want to come with you if you're thinking of emigrating. I've known situations where children have opted to stay in their home country to continue their education and other cases where they couldn't face leaving a girlfriend or boyfriend. I also have relatives whose children have moved to the other side of the world in pursuit of a new way of life. These are not easy situations to work through. Heartache and tears are often present but with love, patience and understanding a way forward can be found.

When you are considering a major change, try to explain your motives. People are usually more accepting once they understand what it is you're trying to do and why. If you are planning to uproot your family, try to find ways that the experience will benefit them also. They might find it hard to appreciate what you're trying to do at this stage but hopefully one day they will look back and realize why you gave up the comfort and security of your current way of life in pursuit of something greater.

Regarding parents, it's great when they're right there with you and lend their support as you take steps forward. However, some parents struggle. I believe we should respect our parents but that doesn't mean you should let them dissuade you from pursuing your purpose – especially once you've grown up and left home. If your parents are struggling to come to terms with your vision, reassure them of your love and respect for them and ask them to try to see things from your perspective. In many cases, with time, they often come around.

EXERCISE: Building your support team

Have you worked out who you want in your support team yet? Would your team include friends and family? How about a coach, mentor or other support group? If you're launching a new business venture have you found a suitable financial and legal advisor? If you've not done this yet, it could be worth investing a bit of time to work out who you need in your support team.

> **Key thoughts to take away:**
>
> This final step has sought to prepare you for some of the challenges you may face as you set off in pursuit of your purpose. Summing up this final step, key thoughts to take away are:

STEP 7: PREPARE FOR SUCCESS

- Appreciate the progress you've made so far
- Accept you may feel disorientated as you navigate change
- Clear out clutter and free up time in your life
- Think positive and feed your soul with good things
- Feel the fear and do it anyway
- Reject rejection
- Embrace failure as a friend who guides you on your path to success
- Find support from family, friends, a coach or other support group

You are now equipped with what you need to find your life purpose and live a more successful and happy life. Recognizing and preparing for potential challenges will keep you from being blown off course. Before we finish though, I'd like to offer a few more thoughts that can help you as you seek to live out your life in pursuit of your purpose.

o o o

AFTERWORD

LIVING
EVERY DAY
IN
PURSUIT
OF YOUR
PURPOSE

o o o

AFTERWORD
Living Every Day in Pursuit of Your Purpose

○ ○ ○

"I believe each of us is born with a life purpose. Identifying, acknowledging and honouring this purpose is perhaps the most important action that successful people take. They take the time to understand what they're here to do – and then they pursue that with passion and enthusiasm."

(Jack Canfield – author and speaker)

○ ○ ○

Pursue your purpose with passion

CONTINUALLY REMIND YOURSELF of your mission. What is it you believe you are here on earth to do? Keep a clear picture in your mind of your vision. Stay focused on what you're aiming to achieve. See the value in what you do. This will keep you motivated knowing that what you're doing is worthwhile. Be enthusiastic, not apologetic. Stay excited about what you do. People who are passionate about something get noticed by others. Obey the command of Tony Robbins: "Live with passion!"

Decide to live without regret

Life is shorter than you think. Tomorrow is promised to no one. You can't change the past but you can learn from it. If you've said or done things you regret, face up to it, accept the consequences, apologize if you can, then move on. Don't let past regrets prevent you from doing something purposeful and life-changing with your future.

If there's unfinished business in your life deal with it while you still have the opportunity. Imagine yourself on your deathbed with your nearest and dearest around you. Is there anything you would want to say to them you haven't already said? Why not say it now? Is there anything you had wished you'd done but didn't? Why not make a plan to do it while you can? Make it your aim to reach the end of life and close your eyes for the last time with no regrets left inside you.

Stay flexible

We live in a changing world. We make plans then life happens. Along our journey we meet new people and experience new things. We gain fresh insights that were previously hidden from us. Circumstances open up new opportunities or close doors previously open to us. Such times may be unsettling and potentially disorientating. When you face circumstances beyond your control, battling against them may be futile. At such times you need wisdom. Stay flexible and try praying Reinhold Niebuhr's well-known prayer: "God grant me the serenity to accept the things I cannot change, the courage to change the things I can, and the wisdom to know the difference."

Enjoy the journey, not just the destination

Staying focused on your vision keeps you moving forwards on your journey. But don't forget to smell the roses blossoming by the roadside as you go. Enjoy the present while you're looking forward to the future. Realize that life is not just about what you achieve at the end of the day. Life is also what happens to you along the way. Appreciate the simple pleasures in life. Be thankful for the opportunities you have to help others as you pass through life.

Keep on keeping on

When it comes to pursuing your life purpose don't be surprised if it feels like hard work somewhere along the way. Don't give in when things get tough and you're tempted to give up. Seek out your support team. Find your inner strength. Encourage yourself to stick at it. Remember that success is "one per cent inspiration and ninety-nine per cent perspiration". Listen again to the words of Winston Churchill who inspired hope in the people of Britain when they faced the severest of trials. He said to them all those years ago, and he still says to you now, "Never give in. Never give in. Never, never, never, never... never give in."

o o o

ADDITIONAL RESOURCES

○ ○ ○

IF YOU'VE WORKED THROUGH the seven steps in this book you should have a clearer idea of your unique purpose in life. You would have also created a plan for the future and know what steps to take next. If you want to find out more about some of the things I've talked about then check out the bibliography at the back of this book or visit the following website:

http://www.FindYourLifePurpose.com

If you would like the benefit of additional support to help you find and live out your life purpose, I'd encourage you to try out some life purpose coaching. You can learn more at:

http://www.FindYourLifePurpose.com/Coaching

○ ○ ○

ABOUT THE AUTHOR

○ ○ ○

MERVYN SMALLWOOD is a life coach and writer who specializes in helping people find and live out their unique purpose in life. Over the years he has taught, coached and supported many people, either one-to-one or in small groups. In 2001 Mervyn and his wife Lynn relocated to West Cornwall in pursuit of a different way of life shortly after the birth of their second daughter. As well as writing he also enjoys walking along the beautiful Cornish beaches and building cafe racer motorcycles.

Having a wide variety of interests, during his life he has been a championship-winning motorcycle racer, achieved runner-up in a national Mechanic of The Year competition, taught himself to ride a unicycle, renovated three houses, and been ordained as a church minister. Addicted to learning, he also has two Masters Degrees and an Advanced Diploma in Life Coaching.

His encouragement to you:

"Your life is precious so learn to appreciate and value it. Who you are and what you do is important. You can touch lives and make this world a better place. Make the effort to discover your purpose and aim to do something worthwhile with your life. Pursue your dream and encourage others to do so also. To your happiness and success..."

Learn more about Mervyn by visiting:
http://www.MervynSmallwood.com

Learn more about life purpose coaching at:
http://www.FindYourLifePurpose.com/Coaching

○ ○ ○

ACKNOWLEDGEMENTS

○ ○ ○

THERE ARE MANY who have played a part in helping this book come into being. First and foremost I'd like to thank my wife, Lynn. It's been her patient and persistent encouragement that's enabled me to keep going so that you actually have a book to read now. Without her, this wouldn't have been possible. I'd also like to thank everyone I've had the opportunity to work with, train and coach over the years, some of whose stories are contained within these pages.

As for professional help, special thanks are due to Susannah Marriot who helped review the initial draft and offered some really useful guidance. Also, thanks to my fellow students in the 2009 Professional Writing group at University College Falmouth for their peer feedback and encouragement. Likewise, thanks also to Alison Rayner for her patient and professional support in providing the cover design, layout and typesetting.

I'd also like to thank you, the reader, for taking the initiative to invest in your own personal development. My sincere hope is that this book helps to stimulate your thinking and provides you with some useful tips and tools to help you find and live out your life purpose – the most important thing you could ever do while you're alive on planet earth...

○ ○ ○

BIBLIOGRAPHY

o o o

OVER THE YEARS I've read thousands of books and articles that have had an impact on me and my thinking. The following are some of them that I've referred to within this book. My hope is that they may shed some further light on specific areas that may be of interest to you.

- Blanchard, K. and Bowles, S. (1998) *GUNG HO!: How to Motivate People in Any Organization*. London: Harper Collins Publishers Ltd.

- Canfield, J. and Hansen, M.V. (1999) *Chicken Soup for the Soul: 101 Stories to Open the Heart and Rekindle the Spirit*. London: Vermilion.

- Canfield, J. (2005) *The Success Principles: How to Get From Where You Are to Where You Want to Be*. London: Harper Collins Publishers Ltd.

- Carman, T. (2005) *Strength-Based Teaching: The Affective Teacher, No Child Left Behind*. Lanham: R&L Education.

- Central Intelligence Agency (2009) *The World Factbook*. Washington: The Office of Public Affairs. Available from https://www.cia.gov/library/publications/the-world-factbook/fields/2102.html (24.01.11)

- Chen, S. and Ravallion, M. (2007) *Absolute Poverty Measures for the Developing World, 1981-2004*. Washington: World Bank Development Research Group.

- Common Purpose UK (2004) *Searching for Something: Exploring the Career Traps and Ambitions of Young People*. London: Common Purpose UK. Available from http://www.commonpurpose.org.uk/media/36828/searching_for_something.pdf (21.10.12)

- Covey, S. (1992) *The Seven Habits of Highly Effective People*. London: Simon and Schuster UK Ltd.

BIBLIOGRAPHY

- Covey, S., Merril, A. R. and Merrill R. R. (1997) *First Things First*. London: Simon and Schuster UK Ltd.

- Edwards, K. (2009) *30 Something and Over it: What Happens When You Get Up and Don't Want to Go to Work... Ever Again*. Edinburgh: Mainstream Publishing Company Ltd.

- Estrine S. and Estrine J. (1999) *Midlife, a Manual*. Boston: Element Books Inc.

- Falk, E., Raybin, N. and Rooney, P. (2010) *Giving USA 2010: The Annual Report on Philanthropy for the Year 2009*. Indiana: Indiana University Center on Philanthropy.

- Gardner, H. (1993) *Frames of Mind: The Theory of Multiple Intelligences*. Waukegan: Fontana Press.

- Gerhardt, S. (2010) *The Selfish Society: How We All Forgot to Love One Another and Made Money Instead*. London: Simon and Schuster UK Ltd.

- Ibarra, H. (2002) 'Managing Yourself: How to Stay Stuck in the Wrong Career', in *Harvard Business Review*. December 2002, pp. 40-47.

- Hill, N. and Stone, W. C. (2007) *Success through a Positive Mental Attitude*. New York: Pocket Books.

- Hume, R. (2007) *The World's Living Religions*. Johannesburg: Crest Publishing House.

- International Bible Society (1973) *Holy Bible, New International Version*. London: Hodder and Stoughton.

- Jeffers, S. (2012) *Feel the Fear and Do It Anyway*. London: Vermilion.

- Leary-Joyce, J. (2009) *The Psychology of Success: Secrets of Serial Achievement*. Harlow: Pearson Education Limited.

- Maxwell, J. (2002) *Your Roadmap for Success: You Can Get There From Here*. Nashville: Thomas Nelson.

- McGraw, P. (2004) *Family First: Your Step-by-Step Plan for Creating a Phenomenal Family*. London: Simon and Schuster UK Ltd.

- Merril, A. and Merril, R. (2003) *Life Matters: Creating a Dynamic Balance of Work, Family, Time and Money*. New York: McGraw-Hill.

- Mill, J. S. (1863) *Utilitarianism*. Brighton: BLTC Research. Available from http://www.utilitarianism.com/mill2.htm (20.12.10).

- Peck, M. S. (1990) *The Road Less Travelled*. London: Arrow Books.

- Pfieffer, C., Vos, H. and Rea, J. (1975) *Wycliffe Bible Encyclopedia*. Chicago: Moody Press.

- Royal Bank of Scotland (2011) *The RBS SE100 Data Report: Charting the Growth and Impact of the UK's Top Social Businesses*. London: RBS Community Banking.

- Salovey, P. and Mayer, J. (2004) *Emotional Intelligence: Key Readings on the Mayer and Salovey Model*. New York: Dude Publishing.

- Sanchez, O. A. (2009) *The Global Arms Trade: Strengthening International Regulations*. [www] http://hir.harvard.edu/climate-change/the-global-arms-trade (30.11.12).

- Smith, K. C. (2007) *The Top 10 Habits of Millionaires: Transform Your Thinking – and Get Rich*. London: Piatkus Books.

- Stone, W. C. (2012) *Believe and Achieve*. Wise: The Napoleon Hill Foundation.

- Tieger, P. and Barron-Tieger, B. (2007) *Do What You Are: Discover the Perfect Career for You Through the Secrets of Personality Type* (4th Rev Ed). New York: Hachette Book Group USA.

- United Nations University (2007) *The World Distribution of Household Wealth*. Helsinki: World Institute for Development Economics Research. Available from http://escholarship.org/uc/item/3jv048hx (03.01.11).

BIBLIOGRAPHY

- University of Warwick (2010) 'Happiness Levels Falling in Europe: Experts Urge Governments to Respond', in *British Journal of Industrial Relations*. 48:4 December 2010 0007-1080 pp. 651-669.

- Vujicic, N. (2010) *Life Without Limits: Inspiration for a Ridiculously Good Life*. New York: Doubleday Religion.

- Wallace, I. (2011) *The Top 100 Dreams: The Dreams that We All Have and What They Really Mean*. London: Hay House UK Ltd.

o o o

If you've got something out of this book why not recommend it to a friend? They will thank you for it. If you've got a story to tell then I'd love to hear from you. Perhaps I could include it in a future edition. If you could spare a few minutes, I'd also greatly appreciate it if you could write a brief review on Amazon for me.

o o o

Printed in Great Britain
by Amazon